Early History of Columbiana, Ohio
1805-1912

Early History of Columbiana, Ohio
1805-1912

Chauncey E. Wolfgang

Commonwealth Book Company
St. Martin, Ohio
2016

Copyright © 1912 by Chauncey E. Wolfgang
Copyright © 2016 by Commonwealth Book Company, Inc.
All rights reserved. Printed in the United States of America.

Preface

A book without a preface is considered very incomplete. So is a ship without a figure-head. In either case the affixture is more ornamental than useful. A book without a preface is nevertheless a book, and a ship without a figure-head is nevertheless a ship. So now in conformity to custom, for custom it surely is, which has existed from time immemorial, we are reminded that a custom makes law, and law must be obeyed. I therefore submit to my readers the following.

In presenting this book to you, the author endeavors to present the facts and nothing but the facts, just as they have been presented to him.

With great care, data has been gathered and assembled in order that this publication can not fail to result in benefit to the community.

This book is not perfect, no man ever saw one that was, but the author consoles himself with the reflection that he has done the best he could under the circumstances, sparing neither time nor expense in getting at the facts underlying the subject treated.

The author's whole aim in this effort was to gain knowledge and impart the information to those who are interested in Columbiana, their home town. It is nothing more than natural that we should be supremely interested in the home town, we once knew so well.

'Twas indeed a gratifying pleasure to note the ready response of the citizens, as they were approached at different times in order to gather the required data for the book. So, one and all, if you please, accept the many thanks the author extends to you, who so kindly assisted him.

These pages are based entirely on the historical records, which have been presented, and no claim is layed to supposition.

CHAUNCEY E. WOLFGANG.

CHAUNCEY E. WOLFGANG

Introduction

The small city of Columbiana, Ohio, has an exceedingly fine location, on the main line of the Pittsburg, Fort Wayne and Chicago Railroad, on sections 3, 4, 9, 10. From the north the Youngstown and Southern trolley line enters our corporate limits and winds its way to Leetonia, our neighboring town, just three miles west.

Columbiana's territorial limits embrace one square mile of land. Her growth has been of a solid, sturdy nature, which always denotes a strong constitution. So, practically, her age has not been against her. The growth was slow and unimportant until the railroad came through; since then its population and material interests have greatly increased.

Columbiana contains the following: The Enterprise Maanufacturing Co., The Columbiana Pump Co., The Brungard Milling Co., The Columbiana Boiler Works, The Columbiana Manufacturing Co., the Banner Manufacturing Co., The Columbiana Lumber Co., Coyle Bros. Grain Elevator, Beard's Basket Works, Zimmer and Harmon Carriage Works, The Auto Machine Co.; several good garages, five churches, a fine high school building, a water works and electric light plant, which is owned by the municipality; fifty-five arc street lamps, between 20,000 to 25,000 feet of water piping within the corporate limits. Has about one mile and a quarter of paved streets, many handsome residences, about 2,000 inhabitants; has the West Virginia gas for lighting and heating, and is the trade center for miles around.

Kilbourne says: "Columbiana is a fancy name taken from Columbus and Anna.

Pending its adoption in the legislature a member facitiously moved to add the name Maria thereto so as to have it read Columbiana Maria. But the legislatule adopted the name Columbiana.

Early History of Columbiana, Ohio

Let us imagine ourselves standing on the public square of Columbiana, Ohio, in June, 1802.

Ah! Nothing but stately oaks on every side, with ever and anon the chirp of some wild bird, the drum of the pheasant, or the clatter of the squirrels as they flit from tree to tree, or branch to branch, as if to break the monotony of the scenes. Such, no doubt, was the panoramic view of Columbiana as seen by Joshua Dixon, who, with his family of a wife and eleven children, located on section 4, in 1802, and built their cabin. A few years later they erected a large brick dwelling on the property where G. Ed. Buzard now lives, and purchased adjoining sections 3 and 4 from the United States Government. On December 15, 1803, their daughter Rachel was married to Benjamin Hanna, a neighbor's son, who lived on section 10, on the place which is now known as the Poulton farm.

The marriage was solemnized according to the custom of the Friends, in the Middleton meeting house. This was the second marriage in the township.

1804

In 1804 John Michael Esterly, with his family, accompanied by a brother, located on section 5, which he bought of the United States Government.

1805

In the fall of 1805 the village of Columbiana was laid out, history tells us, by Joshua Dixon, on the 21st of August, 1805, and embraced originally fifty-eight lots on the southwest quarter of section 4. These lots were located on two streets sixty feet wide, viz.: Main street, 1440 feet in length, and Main Cross street, 1060 feet in length, running with the cardinal points of the compass, and intersecting each other in the center of the square near the top of a hill. The survey of these fifty-eight lots and two streets was made, at this time, by William Heald, a surveyor, under whose direction the greater part of the county was subsequently surveyed.

The main street was located on the later stage route between Pittsburg, Pa., and Wooster, Ohio, through East Fairfield, Ohio. The plat was recorded August 22, 1805, after which time the lots were offered for sale at $25 and $30 each, according to location.

A number of additions have been made to the original plat, the principal ones have been John Todd's on the south, and Sturgeon's on the west. Other lots for village purposes have been added by Deemer, Stouffer and Lamb, Koch, Zeigler, W. E. and A. Sturgeon, Stiver Bros., Roninnger, Wm. Nichols, Mary A. Todd, Betz, Snyder; Nichols and Allen, John Stiver, Joseph and Wm. Wallace, Strickler, Rohrbaugh, Erwin, Vogleson, Holloway, Bell, Allen, Nichols, and Harrold.

1808

In 1808 Michael Croxen built a log tavern on the southwest corner of the public square and Main Cross street, which is now known as West Park avenue. About this time, it is said, Ganar Pierce, a blacksmith, located in the end room of a log building on the northeast corner of the public square and Main street.

1809

The new families who had erected log cabins for homes along the stage route soon called for needed attention concerning the transportation of their heretofore much-delayed mail. So, some time in 1809, the first post-office was established in the home of John Dixon, on the northeast corner of the public square and Main street, with mail being supplied from the East Fairfield office on the stage route line. East Fairfield was founded in the year 1803 and mail had been served at that point for some time.

1812

Joseph Beal built a log cabin in 1812 on the east side of the then known north end of Main street, on the lot where Charles D. Strickler's handsome residence now stands.

1813

About 1813 a Reformed missionary from the east, whose name was Mannesmith, visited Columbiana and held catechetical instructions in the primitive log hotel on the public square. Abraham Fox and Christian Streaby built a small brick building on the northeast corner of Main street and the public square this same year, in which Messrs. Jesse Allen and Benjamin Hanna started in the mercantile business, under the firm name of Jesse Allen and Co. They occupied this small building until 1816, when Benjamin Hanna retired from the firm, leaving Mr. Allen as sole proprietor of the business. Mr. Allen, after a number of years attending closely to business, found his trade had increased to such an extent that more floor space was in great demand. He susbsequently built and occupied the brick structure, which still stands, on the northwest corner of Main street and the public square. He carried on a successful business in this place for many years. Later, deciding to embark in the milling business, he sold his store to his brother-in-law, John E. Icenhour, and bought Hatcher's steam grist mill, which was located about five miles east one one hundred acres of land. Here his misfortune overtook him and he, soon after the death of his wife, moved to Salem, Ohio.

JESSE ALLEN

1814

In August, 1814, the "School and Meeting-House Society" of Columbiana was organized. The purpose of this society was to erect a building on a suitable site to meet the increasing demands of both church and school.

This year Christopher Hively put up a log cabin on what is now the

Blecher property, on the northwest corner of Main street and Mulberry alley. Jacob Harmon also built a log house on what is now the Emit Coblentz corner, which is located on the southeast corner of Main street and the public square.

1815

In 1815 a house of hewed logs was built on the ground now occupied by the Grace church, by the society formed the year before, for the purpose of church and school. In this building the first school in our town was opened, soon after completion. Michael Seachrist built a log building this year, on the lot where the post-office building now stands, on the southeast corner of Main street and Mulberry alley.

1818

In 1818 Ab. Batton cleared off and put up a cabin on the lot where John Beard's tin store now stands, on the west side of Main street, two doors north of the northwest corner lot on Main and Friend street. Isaac Baughman built a log cabin on the corner property just north of the present post-office building. This year a meeting house was built on the east side of Elm street, where Mr. Royal Conkey's residence now stands. In this house of worship meeting according to the faith of the Orthodox branch of Friends was for a time sustained. The street leading from the west to these grounds was soon after called Friend street, in commemoration of this religious sect.

1820

In the year 1820 Jacob Esterly built a log building on the southeast corner of Main and Friend streets. George Foust built a log cabin on the northeast corner of Main Cross street and the square; this is the lot now occupied by "The Ledger" office building. Michael Croxen built a log cabin on the southeast corner of Main street and the square. David Fox erected a log building on the corner where W. T. Holloway's storeroom now stands. This is now known as the southwest corner of Main and Friend streets. David Bishop built a log domicil on the lot now owned by Mrs. Susan Oberholtzer, which is now known as the northeast corner of Main street and Strawberry alley. Joseph Hisey erected the building on Main Cross street owned today by John Eadler. This year, you can see, the ax, the adz, the saw, and the hammer did a wonderful work transforming the scenes into one of civilization.

1822

In 1822 Jonathan Rukenbrod erected a log cabin farthest north on the east side of Main street, just north of David Bishop. This year the School and Meeting-House society's building was torn down and a Union church, for the use of the Lutheran and Reformed congregations, was completed and dedicated. The house was built of brick and occupied the present site of the Grace Reformed church.

1824

In 1824 Israel Bean put up a log house on the southwest corner of Main street and the public square.

1825

In 1825 Thomas Dixon built on the northwest corner of Main and Friend streets. Wm. Moody opened up a general store this year, in the building that had just been erected north of Jesse Allen's storeroom. Mr. Moody is said to have remained in business only ten years. Mr. Moody erected a building on his property on the north side of the west end of Cross street.

1827

In 1827 Geo. Fishbaugh built a log house on the lot just north of the present Union Banking Co.'s brick block, on the southeast corner of Main street and Spring alley.

Samuel DeHoff put up a log house on the lot opposite Main street from Tidd's store, or where the Union Banking Co.'s building now stands. Gotlieb Koocher built on the lot north of the present Grace church property.

1829

In 1829 Samuel Fitzpatrick built a house on the second lot south from the southwest corner of Main and Friend streets. This is where H. A. Keller's hardware salesroom is located. Geo. DeHoff opened a general store on the west side of Main street above the public square. Jacob Nold erected a water power grist mill two miles west of town. This was the fourth mill on this power.

1830

In 1830 John Sturgeon, of Hanover, Pa., located as a tavern keeper in a building on the lot now owned by W. R. Knowles. He soon bought the Caleb Roller place on the public square. It seems that Caleb Roller bought Michael Croxen's log hotel on the square and ran the place a year or two, then, as is recorded, sold to Mr. John Sturgeon, who ran it until his death in 1849.

John Sturgeon's Family

The accompanying picture is that of John Sturgeon, with his son Samuel and his wife Elizabeth, better known in later years as Granny Sturgeon, holding baby William in her hands. This is a very valuable picture, for in those days photography was not an acquired art. The picture is a fine production by a most experienced and efficient artist. At this time sittings for a penciled picture was indeed a tiresome and tedious undertaking. For many years the hotel, under Sturgeon's management, was widely and favorably known.

About 1849 this well-known landlord died, and his good wife, Elizabeth, or better known as Granny Sturgeon, took charge of the hotel until 1865, when she retired from active business life. Mr. Jacob Greenamyer then bought the property, and in 1870 he rebuilt the hotel, which is the present Park House, run by the present landlady, Mrs. Ella Jamison. In 1830 John Young opened up a small store, in which he sold drugs, in a building where

W. T. Holloway's storeroom building now stands, on the southwest corner of Main and Friend street.

This year Wm. Yates opened up a general drygoods and grocery store. There are located now, three general stores in the village. During the year John McClemens did a small business in the grocery line on the northwest corner lot of Main street and Mulberry alley, now known as Blecher's corner, opposite the alley from Law's drug store. Samuel Brubacher, a cabinet maker, began manufacturing furniture in a building where John Beard's tin store is now located.

1831

Isaac Keister

In 1831 Isaac Keister purchased the house and lot of Wm. Moody on the north side of the west end of Cross street. Here he built a pottery shop and kiln, and began the manufacturing of plain earthen ware. The name of the Keister Pottery was widely known. Mr. Keister, sometime later, took his son David in as partner and they continued the business under the firm name of Isaac Keister and Son for many years. Samuel Huffman erected two buildings, one where Tidd's store now stands and one just south on the next lot, opposite Spring alley.

This year Jacob Hum began making silk hats. Although the implements used in their formation were very crude, yet the articles themselves were very creditable. A number of other hatters plied their trades in Columbiana at different times, viz.: Woodward, Probst, Patterson, Bean, Stacy, Fitzpatrick and Leslie. Dr. Woodward, a hatter, sold his property on the corner of Main street and Mulberry alley, to Jacob Hum for $150.

Jacob Hum

John Vogleson

John Vogleson, a shoemaker, located here this year, 1831, and embarked in the shoe business. Mr. Vogleson was the first to enter this line of trade and his sales soon became remarkably good. He remained in this business for twenty-five years. Mr. Vogleson and Joseph Wallace built a warehouse near the P., F. W. and C. railroad, just east of Elm street. They dealt in general produce for about ten years. He served as justice of the peace in Fairfield township from 1830 to 1839. In 1840 he was mayor of Columbiana. He became a notary public, which position he filled for six years. In 1862 he was elected recorder of the village. Mr. Vogleson has indeed filled a useful life.

1832

In 1832 John E. Icenhour, of Damascus, Ohio, located here in order to study the mercantile business with his brother-in-law, Jesse Allen. In 1845, when Mr. Allen moved to a farm about five miles east of Columbiana, Mr. J. E. Icenhour became a partner in his general store on the northwest corner of Main street and the public square, under the firm name of Icenhour and Allen. In 1852 the business was disposed of and they occupied their new building on Main street, north of the railroad, and engaged in the forward and commission business. For a number of years the depot of the P., F. W. and C. railroad was in this building. In 1853 they added a line of drugs, carriage trimmings, hardware, paints, and oils. The firm name was now changed to Icenhour & Co. In 1875 J. E. Icenhour sold his interests in the store to his partner and bought and sold wool, etc., in large quantities. Mr. Icenhour was the Adams Express agent for a number of years.

John E. Icenhour

John Sturgeon, the hotelkeeper, operated a brick kiln about where Union street is now located.

John Fitzpatrick

In 1832 John Fitzpatrick settled and built on the northeast corner lot on Main and Friend streets. This year a frame schoolhouse was erected on the southeast corner of Elm and Main streets.

1833

In 1833 Emanuel Brubaker built on a lot on the east side of Main street, where Shasteen and Fitzpatrick Bros. are now located in the Odd Fellows' building. This is the second lot south on the southeast corner of Main and Friend streets.

Conrad Sponseller began business in the blacksmith trade in a building on Main street, just south of Mulberry alley.

1834

In 1834 Daniel Stouffer located here and began his trade of making shoes. He soon gained a respectable trade for hand-made boots and shoes, and for two years Mr. Stouffer was a very busy man, for as yet he was the second here in this line of trade. Sheets and Holms had a stove foundry on the north side of the east end of Main Cross street, which was afterwards carried on by a Mr. Kingsley. Later the building was converted into a blacksmith shop. Dr. Moses Curry, located here. He was the first permanent physician in the place. A frame meeting house was built on a lot now owned by Edward Funkhouser, which was used by the Methodists as a church and the town hall, when necessary, up to 1859, when the present edifice was built. Jacob Beard, a cabinet maker and undertaker, located in the village and plied his trade of making furniture and coffins.

Daniel Stouffer

1835

In 1835 Mathias Rotzel, a weaver, wove coverlids at his home on North Main street, where Dr. Harry Bookwalter's residence now stands. About this time Jacob Anglemyer made spinning wheels in a small building which stood on a lot just opposite. Adam Wise's residence on North Main street. Henry Seachrist built a residence and blacksmith shop on what is now known as the property north of W. F. Basler's Racket store. John Hisey built the house on the northeast corner of Elm and Main Cross streets. William Wallace went into partnership with Jacob Beard and carried on an extensive business for about three years under the firm name of "Beard and Wallace." Mr. Wallace then withdrew from the firm, having his attention drawn to another enterprise; this left Mr. Beard alone. He continued the cabinet making and undertaking until the year 1862. This year, 1835, Samuel Nichols and Lot Holms formed a partnership and opened a general store in a building on the southeast corner of Main street and the public square. John Winch, a carriage maker, located on West Cross street and built a house on the property now owned by the Havil sisters. He also built a shop on the southwest corner of this plot. In this wood-work shop Simon Roninger learned his trade. Andy Whisler and Anthony Hardman formed a partnership and opened up a general store on the northeast corner of Main cross street and the Public Square. This they continued until about 1840. In 1835 William Potts located here and opened up a small grocery store, on the southwest corner of Main street and Mulberry alley.

Jacob Beard

1836

In 1836 Daniel Stouffer, a shoemaker, opened a general store and placed his brother, David, in the shoe shop to carry on that line of trade. Mr. Stouffer placed a large line of dry goods and groceries on sale in his store and trade increased immediately.

1837

On May 27th, 1837, the first election for village officers was held, under the recently acquired charter of incorporation, in the hotel of John Sturgeon. Twenty-one votes were polled. William Hickman was declared mayor.

Dr. Geo. Metzger

This year, 1837, George Metzger graduated from The University of Pennsylvania, and located at Warrenton, Missouri. Here he resided for several months. He often referred humorously to the time he lived there as being in the "State of Misery." He located in Columbiana on the northwest corner of Main street and Strawberry alley, and was for many years a very successful physician. During the Civil war he was one of the noble band of surgeons in a Cincinnati hospital. At home he was always ready to go when called for. The last summons came for him on Sunday, July 5, 1885.

1838

In 1838 the second election for village officers was held. At this election Samuel Seachrist was declared mayor. James Woods located on the lot now owned by Chas. Strickler and began at his trade of blacksmithing. This year William Potts sold his grocery store to Christopher Hively. Mr. Potts then put in a line of drygoods at his home on the north side of West Cross street, where Gus. Weller now lives, and ran the store until his death in 1839. Peter Kleckner, who was our first cooper, located on his property on West Cross street, now owned by Mrs. Elizabeth K. Wolffang, and built a house and a cooper shop. He subsequently dug a well, and near the well he planted an apple tree. This tree, although seventy-four years of age, is still in vigorous growth. Its trunk now measures eight feet, seven inches in circumference at its base, and six feet, seven inches, six feet from the ground. This tree still bears some apples every year.

Jim Woods, a blacksmith, located and built a blacksmith shop on the east side of North Main street, on the lot now owned by Chas. D. Strickler.

This year J. J. Schauwecker bought the Joseph McClunn tannery and farm from a Mr. Betz, and began the tanning of hides on a much larger scale. Mr. Schauweker's trade was large and his fine leather soon gave his tannery a good reputation.

1839

In 1839 the third election was held. John G. Young was declared mayor. This year the name of Cross street was changed by our city fathers to East and West Cross street. John Young opened rooms in a building on Main street, about where Tidd's Bargain House is now located, and sold drugs.

1840

In 1840 the fourth election for village officers was held. John Vogleson was declared mayor. This year a hook and ladder company was formed.

There were ten men in this company, and they bound themselves with the following oath: "We will fight fire and save property from that destructive element to the best of our ability." This year the air was enlivened by the music of a brass band, just organized by local talent, and was composed of eleven members. John Piert owned and operated a brickyard on the north side of the east end of East Cross street. Abe Kridler has been in the blacksmithing business on the lot now owned by Mrs. Elizabeth Groner for a number of years. Columbiana has 273 inhabitants. Mr. Richard Davis married Mrs. Wm. Potts, and buying Whistler and Hardman's general store, they kept store on the northeast corner of East Cross street and the public square until 1843, when they sold out to Joseph Wallace.

1841
In 1841 Jesse M. Allen built a commodious brick storeroom and dwelling combined, on the northwest corner of West Cross street and the public square.

1842
In 1842 an agreement was had with the County Commissioners, and the village charter was surrendered. The prevailing thought was to attempt the curtailing of expenses.

1843
In 1843 Joseph Wallace opened a general store on the northeast corner of East Cross street and the public square.

1844
In 1844 Joseph Wallace's entire block on the public square burned down, while he was away taking a drove of horses to the Philadelphia market. The block consisted of his dwelling, storeroom, and a large smoke-house, in which the fire originated. Mr. Wallace would take whole wagon loads of smoked meat to the Pittsburg market, and a large smoke-house was really necessary. Excitement reigned supreme, for this was Columbiana's first large fire. The hook and ladder laddies did all they could, but the fire had gained too much of a start. Jacob Greenamyer, a clerk in the store, had saved a quantity of the goods from the storeroom, and upon Mr. Wallace's return, bought these and opened up a store on the southeast corner of Main street and the public square.

Enos Woods this years bought his brother's blacksmith shop on Main street and, building a foundry, he soon made the first steam engines to be manufactured in the village. His machine shop was known far and wide. J. J. Schauweker bought one of these engines and added steam power to his bark mill department in his tannery.

1845
In the summer of 1845 Joseph Wallace erected the building on the corner, in which the "Ledger" is published today. He placed in a line of wool, flaxseed, cloverseed, and grain of all kinds, and did a flourishing business. This year Jacob Flickinger started in the carriage making business on the north side of East Cross street. A Mr. Woodruff opened up a tailoring establishment.

In 1845 Reuben and Joseph Strickler built a small shop on Main street, a few doors from the public square, and began the manufacture of mortising machines.

Their means and machinery were limited, and to get a sale for their manufactured product, they peddled their mortising machine over the country in a one-horse wagon. Reuben invented another machine, known as the "Strickler Boring Machine." This machine is so satisfactory and so simple in construction that no improvement has been made on it since. In order to make this boring machine they were compelled to have an iron planer, but not being wealthy enough to buy one, Reuben made the patterns and they got up the first iron planer between Pittsburg and Mansfield. This proved to be quite a curiosity to the people in and about Columbiana. In order to meet the demand for their goods they were compelled to have a more extensive manufacturing business. A good-sized machine shop and foundry was erected on a vacant lot on the south side of Railroad street in 1848. This year their brother Noah came into the firm and they did a successful business.

Reuben Strickler

The firm manufactured portable cider mills and presses, grai drills, portable sawing machines, sulky hay rakes, besides their boring machine, and carried on a good business until 1866, when they sold their factory and retired from that business.

1846

December 18, 1828, Simon Roninger was born in Hokensville, Chester County, Pa. He and his brother George walked to Columbiana in 1846, having heard of this locality as a promising place to locate, and became an apprentice in April, learning the carriage making trade under John Winch. December 26, 1852, Mr. Roninger married Miss Caroline Sponseller. Three children were born to them, one boy and two girls. The boy died when but a few months old. The two grils' names are: Albesena and Mary Ellen. In 1855 Mr. Roninger built a carriage shop on his own lot on West Cross street, or what is now known as West Park avenue, and made buggies and wagons. He is a well-preserved man for his age, with

Simon Roninger.

a wonderful memory. Mr. Roninger has helped the author on many occasions in gathering data and that person, feeling under grateful obligations, takes this means of sincerely thanking him for his ever kind, able, and most efficient assistance.

In 1846 the frame school building erected on Elm street in 1832 was razed to the ground, and preparations were at once made for the using of this site for a more commodious school building. This building was completed this year, and was a one-story, two-roomed structure. In this house of learning the Columbiana school was continuel until the building was destroyed by fire in 1860. In 1846 Mr. Woodruff, a tailor, took Lot Holms in as partner, and together they continued Woodruff's tailoring establishment. They were said to be neat and tasty and turned out excellent work in their line.

1847

In 1847 a Mr. Skinner located in the building on the southeast corner of Main street and the public square, which is now owned by E. S. Coblentz, and started into the grocery business. This store lasted about three or four years.

1848

Mrs. Sallie Boyer

In 1848 Mrs. Sallie Boyer located in a building on the north side of East Cross street and opened up a small store in her home, where she made the school children's hearts glad by selling them home-made taffies and candies and great sheets of home-baked ginger bread. Mrs. Boyer was the first person in the village to offer roses for sale and many other rare plants.

1850

In 1850 Edward Piert owned and operated two separate brickyards, one on East Cross street and one about where the Pump works now stands.

Lewis (Squire) Wallace, a colored exhorter, and our first home missionary, made religious speeches in Morgan Freed's blacksmith shop.

1851

April 2, 1828, John S. Metzger received his diploma from Nathaniel T. Potter, president of the University of Maryland. In June, 1828, he located at Marlesburg among the mountains of Huntingdon county, Pa. On one occasion a guide was sent to take him to see a sick man living on the mountain side. After riding about four miles on good roads they came to a house and barn by the roadside. The guide said, "We dismount here. I will give you a lantern, and tell you the way to go." The doctor flung his saddlebags over his shoulder and started on his long walk. At some distance up the ascent he was met by a large dog, who took the fingers of his disengaged hand in his mouth and so trotted beside him until they reached the door of the cabin. October, 1851, Mr. Metzger located with his family in Columbiana and assisted his brother in his practice for some years. Saturday, October 1, 1881, he entered the "Land of Leal."

This year Rev. Henry Kurtz began the publication of the "Gospel Visitor" in the springhouse on his father's farm near Haas' schoolhouse, northeast of the village. This publication was devoted to the interests of the society of Dunkards, of which he was a member. David Havil built a blacksmith shop on his lot on the northwest corner of West alley and the west end of West Cross street and commenced at the blacksmith trade, which he bought from John Winch. A Mr. Wolf, a tin and copper smith, located a shop on the west side of Main street north of the recently surveyed route of the P., F. W. & C. railroad, about where Isaih Flickinger's residence now stands. He had a large sale for his copperware, which was hand-made and of the best material.

Dr. John S. Metzger

1852

In 1852 the Pittsburg, Fort Wayne and Chicago railroad was opened through the township for passenger and freight transportation. Columbiana was one of the stations along the route, with Aaron Pile first station agent in the place. Geo. Lamb and Henry Hephner was a tailoring firm about this time.

About April, Richard Davis located in a frame building on Main street, north of Spring alley, and opened up a general store on the spot where J. J. Fesler's grocery store is now. Later Mr. Davis put in a line of drugs and devoted his attention to the sale of this commodity.

John Vogleson and Joseph Wallace built a warehouse on the lot located on the northeast corner of Elm street and the P., F. W. and C. railroad. This was afterwards known as the Rea &

Richard Davis

Powell warehouse. They dealt in general produce. The tailoring firm of Hosey & Hephner was plying its trade here this year. Mr. Hephner later became a partner to Jesse Erwin in the drygoods business.

1853

In 1853 David Havil accepted Lafayette Stuckman as partner in the blacksmith business and they bought a large building at Oiltown and moved it onto Mr. Havil's lot on W. Cross street and did blacksmithing on an extensive scale.

Isaac Esterly opened up a drygoods and grocery store on the corner of Main and Railroad streets. Glosser & Holloway opened up a hardware store in the building on the southeast corner of Main street and the public square. Samuel Brubaker sold his cabinet shop to his son Lorenze, who continued the business of his father. He later moved to a vacant room on what is now known as the Mrs. Malinda Shingler's property on Main street. He had his home in the brick building opposite, which is now owned and occupied by Mr. Harley Shillinger. Henry Blecher opened up a confectionery store in his home on Main street.

Havil and Stuckman

1854

January 10, 1854, The Union Line Express Co. began business at the different towns along the P., F. W. & C. R. R. Their first weighbill from Columbiana reads as follows:

No. 1.

4 pkgs. 665 lbs. Shipped by Icenhour and Allen, to

Wick and McCandless,

Pittsburg, Pa.

The Union Line Express Co. continued in business here until 1856.

In 1854 Valentine Hinkle opened up a restaurant, where he sold drinks in connection, in a building on the east side of Main street, where Mrs. Mary Kromer now resides.

In 1854 Geo. G. Webb, of Greenford, Ohio, bought a large Degaratype wagon and began making pictures. He was the first man in the state to make pictures. After remaining there about one year the car was removed to Enon Valley, where Mr. Webb made pictures for some time. At last he decided to look about for a place suitable for a permanent location. He then drove his wagon through Petersburg and New Springfield, and not being at all satisfied with the trade outlook for his line, he arrived here in 1858 and stopped on the public square. Some time in 1857 a Mr. Manley and R. G. Carpenter constructed a similar wagon to Mr. Webb's and began taking pictures, but not liking the work, Mr. Manley soon sold to Mr. Carpenter and left town. Mr. Carpenter a few weeks later quit the business. Mr. Webb finding his trade in this village growing, and being impressed with the place, decided to locate here. A room was remodeled to his liking as to light and beauty over Valentine Hinckle's restaurant, and here for many years he produced the best of work. This book is illustrated with reproductions of many daguerreotypes of his early production.

Geo. G. Webb

Mr. Webb moved his family, whom he had left in Greenford, to Columbiana in 1861.

1855

In 1855 Moses Coblentz and David Sprinkle opened up a general store at the southwest corner of Main and Friend streets. David Sprinkle some time later sold his interest in the store to Amos Sprinkle, thus leaving the firm name stille Coblentz and Sprinkle. This year Mr. Henry Blecker died and his wife, Jane, or better known as Granny Blecker, continued the confectionery business for many years.

Johnnie Myers, a weaver, located in a building on the east side of Main street, on the northwest corner of the property now owned by Miss Julia Wolf.

Secret Society—Allen Lodge No. 276, F. and A. M.

August 1, 1855, Allen Lodge No. 276, F. and A. M. of Columbiana, Ohio, was chartered on petition of the following persons: Geo. Lamb, D. K. Bertolette, John C. Ansley, R. H. Carpenter, John E. Allen, Benjamin Allen, Moses Mendurhall, Lewis W. Vale, Thomas C. Allen, John Baker, Allen Coulson, Philip Fetzer, and John L. D. Heinman. D. K. Bertolette was elected the first master; John C. Ansley, Senior Warden; and R. H. Carpenter, Junior Warden. Regular meetings of the lodge have since been held. There have been 166 members, but deaths, removals and the formation of lodges at East Palestine and Leetonia have reduced the membership to 95.

Officers for 1912: C. V. Calvin, W. M.; Roy E. Weaver, S. W.; H. A. Inman, J. W.; Isaiah Flickinger, treasurer; John Barrow, secretary; C. E. Beard, S. D.; Dick Fitzpatrick, J. D.; John A. Wingard, Tyler; John W. Moore, chaplain. Trustees: Fred Thoman, three years; John Barrow, two years; Roy E. Weaver, one year. Grievance Committee: John W. Holloway, J. J. Fesler, A. C. Bell. Stewards: Eli Flickinger, S. S.; R. E. Lodge, J. S.

1856

Before the grading and improving of Main street that thoroughfare, from the P., F. W. and C. R. R. to the public square, was a continuation of hillocks. For the convenience of pedestrians, steps were constructed at the necessary places on the sidewalks. As late as 1856 about twelve steps were known to have existed in the distance from the railroad to the public square.

December 3, 1856, the Union Line Express Co. was succeeded at this place by the Adams Express Co. This Express Co. continued in business until 1857.

In April, 1856, history tells us that this locality was visited by the worst storm the oldest citizen can recall. Its duration was only a few hours, but the havoc wrought to this community was great. Houses were unroofed and moved on their foundations, others being completely overturned. Whole orchards were lowered to the ground, while great trees were compeletly uprooted. Then the rain that followed caused the dams and bridges to be washed away. The newly laid tracks of the P., F. W. and C. Railroad were severely damaged, and in many places the tracks were washed from their foundations. This kind of a storm is a common occurence in the far western states, but this certainly was an unusual occurrence for old Columbiana.

In 1856 John D. King, attorney-at-law, located here. Twice Columbiana has had lawyers (W. W. Orr and Wm. McLaughlin) to locate within her borders, but in turn they left the field of labor to search for more promising spots where they could the better and sooner achieve success in their profession. Havil and Stuckman, who had for several years been engaged in the blacksmith trade in their shop on the north side of West Cross street, this year dissolved partnership. Mr. Stuckman then built a new blacksmith shop at the west end of his lot, and taking his brother, Daniel, in as a partner, they worked together for a number of years. Mr. Havil at this time accepted his son, Isaac, as partner in his work, and they carried on business under the firm name of Havil & Son. For more than fourteen years the village had been unincorporated, but on the 9th day of June the county commissioners granted a new charter, whose powers extended to the same limits as the former charter.

1857

On April 14, 1857, a borough election was held. Forty-eight votes were polled. George Lamb was declared elected mayor. A. C. Bell, Sr., succeeded Aaron Pile as station agent, at Columbiana, of the P., F. W. & C. railroad.

The office of "The Gospel Visitor," a small German and English publication devoted to the interests of the society of Dunkards, was moved from the rooms on the Kurtz farm to the village. This printing office was located in the northwest rooms of the house located on the northeast corner of Main street and the public square. This was the home of this monthly publication for nine years. A telegraph office was opened in the Pittsburg, Fort Wayne & Chicago railway company's office in Columbiana this year, with A. C. Bell, Jr., as operator.

1858

In 1858 the Strickler brothers began the manufacturing of a boring and mortising machine, invented by Reuben Strickler. School district No. 2 was organized in June of this year, under the act of March 14, 1853, as a special district, with Michael Henry, David Woods and Jacob Greenamyer as the members of the board of education.

In 1857 George Freed conducted a marble works on the present South Main street, with George Frasier employed as marble cutter. Mr. Frasier later conducted a marble works on the northeast corner of Main and railroad streets.

It seems that the Union Line Express Co. regretted the move made in 1856, for that express company again succeeded the Adams Express companay at the Icenhour and Allen office, June 19, 1857. The Union Line Express Co. was now the only carrier of express to Columbiana until 1868.

Michael Henry

1859

In 1859 George Roninger became the partner of his brother, Simon, and under the firm name of Roninger Bros. they engaged in the manufacturing of wagons on a large scale. On the 4th and 5th of June occurred what is remembered here as the big frost. It was a memorable Sunday morning when the good people of this locality arose to find that during the night a frost of such magnitude had visited them that every tender vegetable sprout had been blackened and destroyed. Wheat had already grown so tall that the crop was completely ruined. The only redress they had was to replant the corn, and grow buckwheat (a quick maturing cereal, which would ripen before the close of the harvest) that they might have enough to live on that winter. It was a most discouraging situation, but with hope and courage they lived through it all.

This year the present Methodist church was built. It was a fine brick structure and was dedicated by Father Swasey. The building committee was composed of Daniel Deemer, Daniel Stouffer, and Wm. Wright. J. W. Glosser and D. Holloway formed a partnership and opened up a hardware store in a building on the southeast corner of the public square. They continued the business for about two years under the firm name of Glosser & Holloway. This year John Deemer operated a brick yard west of town on the lot now owned by the Beard Stephan & Co., and manufactured the brick used in the construction of the present Methodist Episcopal church, on the southeast corner of Main and Pittsburg streets. Later J. C. Groner operated a brick yard in his field along Mill Creek, just west of town, for many years.

1860

In 1860 the one-story brick schoolhouse, which was built in 1846 on a lot on the northeast corner of Elm and Cross street, caught fire and burned to the ground.

This year the council, on the advisement of Mayor T. C. Allen, decided to change the name of Main Cross street, which crossed the Main street at the public square, to East and West streets.

Robert Close located on Pittsburg street and made brooms for general use. These brooms were said to be A No. 1, and the very best hand-made article ever on the market. He was employed at this trade for many years.

1861

In 1861 Mrs. C. A. Haas taught select school in the room on the second floor of a building owned by Wm. Wallace, on West street. She later, at different times, taught in the Hicksite church and in the basement of the Grace Reformed church.

Ground was broken this year on the northwest corner lot of Pittsburg and Elm streets, preparatory to the erection of a proposed school building.

1862

In 1862 Columbiana was aroused by the great Civil war news that was now crowding the newspaper columns on every hand. Speeches were being made ever and anon; female glee clubs sang patriotic songs, and drum corps music all enstilled in every man's breast the patriot's love for home and country. Already Captain Higgins' company had been formed and in the last days of June, 1861, a regiment, which included "C", was organized at Camp Chase, near Columbus, O. The regiment proceeded to Cheat Mountain, Va., where it arrived August 14, 1861 Now news arrived home direct from the front. Every one was stirred with deep emotion, knowing the prevailing need of quick action. Already two dead bodies had been shipped to dear ones at home by rail to Columbiana, and the year had very little prospective pleasure for anyone who was awaiting so patiently at home for news. Men were enlisting everywhere and Captain Abdiel Sturgeon stoody ready to have his company ("H") filled out. This company eventually joined with the One Hundred and Fifteenth Regiment, and was mustered into the United States service September 18, 1862.

In this year work was begun on the erecting of a school building. Since the destruction of the one-story brick house there was no school held. During this time James Davidson, Mrs. C. A. Haas, Miss Elizabeth Close, and other teachers, were holding select school in different buildings about the village.

Columbiana in 1862
The Carrier's Address

The following lines were written by a Columbiana scribe during the civil war. He signs his name as "Carrier," but his identity is unknown. His poeticability may be questioned, but the mention made of the business interests of Columbiana at that time will be of interest to the readers of this book.

    The earth again has gon around,
      Without discord or jaurring sound;
    To disturb a single sister world,
      Past which we've been so swiftly whirled.

Once more has this planet, thru the realms of space,
  Gone round to the wonted starting place;
And as true as the needle to the pole,
  The Carrier is here to cheer your soul,
And as the hastening years go by,
  And the children of men grow old and die—
Much wrong is done; and bitter pain,
  Is strewn o'er land and the roaring main,
And altho' it is wrong, it must be confessed,
  That the devil has suffered and sinned with the rest.
But you have a remedy, and how it chimes,
  On the ear of one not accustomed to dimes:
And oh! give me in exchange for this,
  A quarter which you will never miss.
Enough of this. A ware is here,
  And patriots, whom all should hold dear,
In the deadly strife and risking their lives,
  To protect their honors, homes, and wives;
While we are at home taking our ease,
  They are standing on guard in mud to their knees,
And many perhaps without a shirt to their back,
  Are striving some southern city to sack,
While we are regaling and having a feast,
  Caring as little for them, as we would for a beast.
Oh! patrons and countrymen, how long will this be so?
  Why not drop everything and say we will go,
And fight for our country, our home, and our flag,
  Compelling secession to give us up Brag?
But Fremont is removed, by the papers I see,
  Because the "niggers" of traitors he declared to be free.
Hurrah for Fremont. Oh! long may he live,
  To enjoy the eulogium which the people will give;
For certainly his plan we all must adopt,
  If from under secession, we would push out the prop.
Scott has resigned, and McClelland's promoted,
  As a military tactician he is bound to be noted;
His gentlemanly bearing for him has secured,
  The respect of an army to hardships inured.
Secession is trembling, and cannote determine,
  The strength of the army gone South under Sherman,
Traitors are quaking down at Bull Run,
  The "Yankees" are anxious and a fight will not shun.
Our navy is mighty; our army is large,
  Come on, my kind patrons, lets on with the charge.
My beloved country we bid you adieu,
  To describe our fair city I dare not eschew.
It is pleasantly located in a beautiful spot,
  The climate is not cold, nor yet is it hot.
We have young men and maidens, who I'm sure will compare
  With the choicest and nicest to be found anywhere.
We don't boast of our churches—having but two—

But they're large and commodious, altho' they're but few.
There's Strickler's Machine Shop and Geo. Smith's steam mill,
And Vogleson's warehouse, which it take a good deal to fill;
There's Allen and Icenhour, with Joe Betz in the brick,
And quite a large drug store to keep people sick.
We have Bell at the station—opposite Holtz's saloon,
Where they serve up fresh oysters at midnight or noon.
Scott keeps a tavern, and a good one, I know,
Where travelers are cared for whenever they go;
And Dave is a "burster"; they say he is strong,
But as he weighs only two hundred, I think they are wrong.
But I must not forget to notice Esterly's store,
For if you buy once there, you're sure to buy more.
But here we're at Hinkle's; well, Mal, how'd you do?
How long will it take to get me up a stew?
Now, as you keep ale, I'll tell you I'm dry,
And I'll not leave your shanty, till my want you supply.
But we next came to Robinson's, who keeps a hotel,
And altho he keeps tavern, he don't keep whiskey to sell.
Then there's Vogleson's shoe store—I came near omitting—
Which certainly would have been wrong; for he can't be beat fitting.
While speaking of shoemakers, I must not omit Troll,
Who may always be found driving his awl.
If your boot needs soleing, take it to Haas,
Or your carriage repairing, they will do it at Inase's.
Beeson lets horses for business or fun,
Geo. Webb takes pictures by the light of the sun;
Wolfe keeps a tin shop and makes copper ware.
The Miss Hoffman's make bonnets for the ladies as fair,
Mark makes matches, as well as he can;
Dr. Steel is a smasher, a bird of a man,
Blecher's keep a grocery, and sell eggs and ale,
And keep out a sign, which says, "Oysters for Sale."
There is Jake Beard and Brubaker, who make coffins and chairs,
And Bill Lane, the barber, who clips off your hairs.
Richard sells medicines, (not Richard the Third),
And the best of tobaccos at Landgraves's, I've heard.
At the post-office is Hiner, who is always so grave,
And if he's not a good postmaster, then I'm a good knave.
And then there's the Ledger, which we all love to read,
To gather its contents, and its precepts to heed:
It is published by Beecher, who is one of the B'hoys,
He always keeps silent, but when making a noise.
Geo. Lamb is our mayor, and a man of good note,
He can make breeches or mend up your coat;
His son, Billy, works with him, who teaches music, they say,
And all his pupils improve, who his directions obey.
If you go to the Fourth Ward, I'm sure you'll find Jake,
Whose business is saddles and harness to make.
And Snyder, the painter, whom you'll find any place,

You surely will know him by the hair on his face.
You'll find Deemer and Metzger, both men-of-the-dead,
And excellent doctors, and very well read;
If anything ails you, they'll give you a pill,
And present to you afterwards a reasonable bill.
There's Sturgeon, the tinnner, (we know him as Bill),
And John, who works with him, but can never be still.
You'll see Stouffer, the merchant (he's a very nice man)
His son you'll find with him, I mean little Dan.
Allen keeps newspapers, and budgets of fun,
If you pay your dues monthly he'll send you no dun.
We now come to Jesse, and Mary, his wife,
They have invested their capital together for life;
They sell goods as cheap as any in town,
So, go in and try them. I'll warrant they'll not frown.
We'll now go down West street and see what we can find,
To tickle the fancy or strengthen the mind.
If we drop in at Simons we're sure to find George,
And hard by you will find Trucksass at work at his forge.
A little below them, you'll find Havil at work,
And from the amount he accomplishes, I conclude he's no shirk.
Groner makes buggies, and Keister makes crocks,
Mrs. Lindsay is a milliner, and sometimes makes frocks.
Granny feeds strangers, and some that are not,
At Joe Wallace's cheap store, goods can be bought.
Down at Mose Coblentz's they keep goods that are fine,
And if you go with money, I'll warrant he'll not whine.
Many of the people have gone off to fight,
And as one of that number, I'll mention Joe Wright.
Then there's Deemer, and Lindsay, and Hively Joe,
All men of good bottom, as we very well know.
Then there's Vogleson, Laughlin, Hauan, and Moore,
Have packed up their knapsacks, and gone off to war.
May success attend them and victory their arms,
And they return safe to their homes and their farms.
Davidson's a teacher of school, I'm told,
And his pupils inform me that he knows how to scold;
As to the truth of the story, I cannot assert,
But if they ever get scolded, it will do them no hurt.
Now patrons and friends, my rhyme's near a close,
That its your quarters I'm after, everyone knows.
And if you don't give it to me, I'll surely commit sin,
For to pay for tobacco, I must now have tin.
Remember this maxim—'tis old, but its true—
"Be sure to give always the Devil his due."
And what is there else, but the root of all evil,
Will make of an innocent carrier a d-l?
Next year perhaps I'll come again,
Good morning, friends; farewell till then.
Truly yours,
THE CARRIER.

1864

About 1864 John Sturgeon embarked in the drygoods business in the building on the southwest corner of Main street and the public square. He was not very successful, so about 1878 the stock was bought by the Gaylor Bros. and he quit the business. This year a political meeting and ox roast was held in the H. H. Beck's grove just west of town. This was the first ox roast Columbiana ever participated in.

1865

April 18, 1865, a memorial service was held in the M. E. church at the same time Abraham Lincoln's funeral service was being enacted in Oak Ridge cemetery, near Springfield, Ill. Rev. Mr. Johnson, a Presbyterian minister of Salem, Ohio, made the funeral address. A number of old citizens gathered at the town hall on East Cross street and, headed by marshall music: Frederick Blecher, fifer; John Wolfe, bass drummer, and Henry Blecher, tenor drummer, they marched to the public square, where a company or armed soldiers joined the procession to the M. E. church. After the services had been concluded they again marched to the town hall, where they disbanded and went to their several homes. Henry Donges was marshall of the day.

This year John Vogleson and son George embarked in the retail business in one of the buildings Mr. Vogleson erected on the lot where the Frederick block now stands. George tended to the sales of the goods, while his father turned his attention to making shoes again, and continued for several years until he retired from actual business life.

Captain Benjamin S. Wright, of the One Hundred and Forty-third Regiment, O. V. I. (National Guard), was buried, under military honors, January 31, 1865. The musicians that played the funeral march to the grave were: Frederick Blecher, fifer; Henry Blecher, tenor drum; John Wolfe, bass drum. Three vollies were fired over the grave. This was the first military burial in Columbiana. Wm. Brenneman located on Railroad street and erected a cooper shop and made baskets, barrels, butter firkins, and tubs.

1866

In 1866 W. W. Wallace of Pittsburgh, Pa., bought the factory owned by the Strickler Brothers and began the manufacturing of the self-discharging hay rake "Welcome." In 1868 the shops were enlarged to four times their original size. In 1870 a large building on the northwest corner of Railroad and Elm streets, connected to the west of the works by an overhead bridge, was built. Farm machinery, stoves, and ranges were then added to the daily output of the factory. A good successful business was carried on until 1877, when fire destroyed the entire plant. Mr. Wallace never rebuilt.

Flickinger's Furniture Factory.

In 1866 Jacob and John Flickinger began the manufacturing of furniture and coffins in a shop on the north side of East Park avenue, and for six years carried on business under the firm name of Flickinger & Son. In 1877 Wm. Flickinger and Solomon Culp erected a two-story frame furniture factory on Pearl street and continued the manufacturing of furniture. In 1883 Jacob Flickinger and sons (Isaiah and Eli), who were running a furniture store on Main street, bought Solomon Culp's interest in the factory on Pearl street and had the works removed to their lot on the southwest corner of Elm street and Mulberry alley. Steam was their motive power. The works employed six men. Fire destroyed the factory in 1891. They never rebuilt.

This year Noah Strickler and Henry Snapp embarked in the manufacturing and sale of boots and shoes, under the firm name of Strickler & Snapp. They had a good trade and for a few months of the eighteen months they were in business, they were compelled to employ no less than eighteen hands.

1867

In 1867 Geo. Buzard and Henry Smith purchased the stock and trade of Coblentz & Sprinkle, and opened a general store under the firm name of Buzard and Smith. They then occupied the southwest corner building on Main and Friend streets. Some time after this, they sold their store to F. P. Farrand, who continued the business in the Farrand block, opposite the M. E. church.

Peter Frason located here and, buying the stock and trade of "Strickler & Snapp," embarked in that business in a building on the southwest corner of Main street and Mulberry alley.

Joseph and Noah Strickler opened up a grocery store under the firm name of J. and N. Strickler.

Jacob F. Staley, a cabinet maker, located on Pittsburg street and began working at his trade with Samuel Brubaker, making furniture.

Samuel Lindsay operated a brick kiln in a field north of town in 1867, about where Mathias Lamonchit's farm is located.

1868

Cemetery

The corporation established a cemetery on the hill at the eastern limits of the village in 1868. The grounds contains eight acres. The minutes of the council proceedings, pertaining to this purchase, is here reproduced in print, and is as follows:

An Ordinance No. 43.

Relating to Cemetery Grounds.

Be it ordained by the Council of the Incorporated Village of Columbiana, Columbiana County, Ohio.

Section 1st. That for the purpose of purchasing grounds for Cemetery purposes, and embellishing the same, it is hereby ordained that a tax of one per cent. per annum for two years be levied upon the taxable property within said Incorporated Village, and also that in addition thereto, there shall be levied a tax of two mills per annum on the dollar on said taxable property for the period of six years, for the same purpose.

Sec. 2nd. This ordinance shall take effect from and after its passage.
Passed April 20th, 1867.

I. T. BARCLAY, Mayor.
I. F. STURGEON, Recorder.

The grounds have been tastefully embellished, and daily are beautified with pains-taking care by the present cemetery sexton, Andrew J. Lindsay.

In 1868 Dr. Abraham S. Sampsell began the practice of medicine.

Secret Societies—Panora Lodge No. 410, I. O. O. F.

Panora Lodge No. 410, I. O. O. F., was organized at Columbiana November 15, 1868, with twenty members and the following officers: A. Sturgeon, Noble Grand; J. T. Barclay, Vice-Grand; A. C. Bell, Recording Secretary; ———, Financial Secretary; T. C. Allen Right Support to Noble Grand; F. Farrand, Left Support to Noble Grand; W. R. Knowles, Right Support to Vice-Grand; Isaac Beeson, Left Support to Vice-Grand; Joe DeHoff, Warden; Dale Stouffer, Treasurer.

At present the officers are: Noble Grand, J. O. Entrikin; Vice-Noble Grand, Zoe Troll; Recording Secretary, D. M. McGaffick; Financial Secretary, F. H. Grove; Treasurer, Jerry Shontz; Right Support to Noble Grand, Jacob Zimmer; Left Support to Noble Grand, Albert Troll; Right Support to Vice-Grand, David Whispel; Left Support to Vice-Grand, Geo. Keyser; Conductor, W. S. Shinn; Warden, Harry Wagner. The lodge at present has about 118 members.

On February 29, 1868, the Adams Express Co. again succeeded the Union Line Express Co. at this place. The Adams Express Co. has now held its position to the present time.

1869

A cider mill was operated just west of town on the Lisbon road in the year 1869 by Joseph Fries for three years. Dr. James Barclay, a dentist, opened dental parlors in the house on the southeast corner of Main street and the public square.

1870

In 1870 Buzard & Smith sold their stock and trade to Cope & Erwin. The business was only continued a few years until Cope sold his share in the store to his partner, who, under the business name of Jesse Erwin, continued until 1883, when he sold his residence and salesroom property to Leonard Holloway, and moving his stock to Alliance he continued there in business many years.

John Vogleson and Jesse Erwin entered into the lumber business under the firm name of Erwin & Vogleson. They carried on their trade on Railroad street.

The first hardware store was opened in a room on North Main street, on the lot owned by Frederick Swartz.

1871

The first saving bank in Columbiana was opened in January, 1871, in the southwest room of the Clark Allen building on the northwest corner of Main street and the public square, by J. H. Hollins and Wm. Kemble. In April Jacob Shamber located on Railroad street and built himself a cooper shop on the property he still owns.

1872

Fire Apparatus of Columbiana, Ohio

On May 20, 1872, an ordinance providing for the appointment of a fire marshal to take charge and keep in repair the hand engine, which the town then owned, and the necessary apparatus to protect the village against fire, was passed. As early as 1840 Columbiana had an orgnization called "Columbiana Fire Company." The apparatus consisted of hooks, ldders, and buckets.

Hope Fire Company was organized at Columbiana July 18, 1884, with Isaih Flickinger as president. The membership totaled twenty-four. July 10, 1888, the constitution was revised and again in 1892.

In 1896, owing to the fact that a new water system had been provided by the town, it was thought proper to reorganize the company and change the constitution, which was approved by the entire membership. Under the new organization the company is known as The Independent Hose Co. No. 1 of Columbiana. The present president is Frank Keyser, and the company is composed of about thirty-one members.

In 1872 Reuben Strickler opened up a general grocery and provision store in the Patterson house. He was the first to introduce the sale of celery. He was known to have said: "The people of Columbiana are very slow in accepting the delicacy. It seems they have to learn to eat it."

This year Henry Beck purchased the property of Joseph Fries and put in a steam power "Boomer" apple cider press instead of the old horse-power press which Mr. Fries had used on the place. He proceeded to embark in the apple cider and vinegar business on a large scale. This mill was run with varying success until 1890, when Mr. Beck abandoned it to give more of his attention to the work on his large and beautiful farm. October 1, 1872, Mrs. F. F. Garrett opened up a millinery store on the east side of Main street, just south of the public square.

Samuel Harrold began blacksmithing in 1872 and worked eighteen years in a shop on Lisbon street.

1873

In 1873 Harry Gates, a harness maker, located in a room in a building on East Cross street and made harness.

At a council meeting August 13, the following resolution was presented: Resolved, that the name of the street running east and west from the public square, and heretofore known by the various names of Potter street, Petersburg street, and Main Cross street be and is hereby changed to Park avenue. This resolution was adopted at this meeting.

Dr. A. L. King, a graduate of the Cincinnati Medical college, engaged in the practice of his profession in a building on Main street and the northeast corner of Spring alley.

A. H. Phillips opened the hotel on the southwest corner of Main and Union streets, and ran the Phillips House for several years.

Wendell Kratz, a weaver, living just north of town, wove coverlids.

1874

Dr. Daniel Deemer settled as a physician in Columbiana on the west side of North Main street. He served two years as county treasurer in 1864-65.

Dr. Enos Greenamyer began practice of medicine in Columbiana.

Frederick Blecher began taking pictures in rooms in Granny Blecher's building on Main street, and on the north side of Mulberry alley.

Miss Allie Slavern, a music teacher, opened rooms for the teaching of music in the Phillips House.

Wm. Deemer and Simon Sprinkle opened up a hardware store on the then South Main street, and dealt in brooms and hardware.

John Koch had a harness shop in a building on the southwest corner of Fairfield avenue and the railroad. He ran this shop a number of years.

About 1874 Henry Tullis and son had a marble works on Union street.

1875

At a council meeting Janury 11, 1875, our city fathers decided the annexation of all the territory embraced in sub-school district number 2 of Fairfield Township not now within the limits of the corporation.

About 1875 J. J. Johnson built a foundry on a lot on the north side of the P., F. W. & C. R. R. tracks and east of Elm street, and began experimenting on some method of turning iron into steel. For years he experimented until, as he thought, the acme of his research had been reached, and he had something like the article which he so much desired. Local blacksmiths said the J. J. Johnson steel was as good as any Norway steel ever produced. It was a crucial moment for him when a day was set and businessmen came from Pittsburg, Pa., to investigate his process. It was rumored that he had been offered $400,000 for the secret, but refused. When Mr. Johnson died, the secret which he had kept so guardedly died with him. In the early 80's he had turned his attention to the manufacturing of artificial gas. This was accomplished by gas being produced by some method of his with crude petroleum. He then became associated with a small corporation which eventually froze him out. This company soon abandoned work indefinately, and the building remained idle until Mr. Johnson's death. It is reported that the corporation then further improved the process and part of the city of Boston is now illuminated with Artificial gas made by the Johnson process.

In 1875 Leonard Holloway and Aaron Overholt bought the general store of Jonathan Esterly. January, 1876, Mr. Holloway bought Mr. Overholt's half interest in the store. For several years he continued in business in the Jonathan Esterly building on the northwest corner lot of Main and Railroad streets. In 1883 he took Jacob Yoder and W. T. Holloway, his son, in as partners. They then purchased the Jesse Erwin buildings, which included the large storeroom on the southwest corner of Main and Friend streets and soon after moved their store to this corner. Here they continued under the firm name of Holloway, Yoder & Co. In 1895 Leonard Holloway died and Jacob Yoder sold his interest to W. T. Holloway. At this same corner he is continuing today a large business under the business name of W. T. Holloway.

In 1875 Dr. J. B. Thompson, homeopathist, located here and began the practice of medicine.

This year the first bank, opened by Hollis and Kemble, was succeeded June 1 by Jonathan Esterly, Abraham Esterly and Augustine Windle, under the firm name of J. Esterly & Co.

Daniel Basler located on a lot on the west side of Middle street, south of Union street, and started in the blacksmithing business, ironing buggies and waggons, and repairing same, until the year 1896.

1876

In 1876 A. C. Bell was elected mayor of Columbiana. Mr. Bell held his office until 1890. He was one of the best mayors ever elected, making many good and lasting improvements. Notable among these was the establishment of the electric light and water plant. He became P., F. W. and C. R. R. agent at the death of his father in 1880. Mr. Bell has held many prominent position in the Masonic lodge. On the night of the capture of the Confederate raider, John Morgan, Mr. Bell, as telegraph operator, was kept busy at the instrument without sleep from Saturday evening until the following Monday.

On the Fourth of July, 1876, the Centennial celebration, which commemorated the signing of the Declaration of Independence, was held in Kyser's grove. Al Bushong, the Indian chief, and his Klu Klux band, on this occasion gathered in Todd's woods, along the south corporation line or what is now known as the woods on the Smith allotment, and lead the parade, which consisted of a fantastically attired company of men, women and children, marching and riding horse back, or on Conestoga wagons, sometimes known as prairie schooners, as floats, loaned by willing parties for the occasion, to Kyser's grove. This was a beautiful spot at that time and well adapted to such picnic gatherings, and was located at the northwest corporation limit. After dinner, which was served in the woods, speeches were made, and in the afternoon they gathered in the public square, where they were entertained by a line of sports such as sack races and balloon ascensions. Jos. Hiner climbed a greased pole of unusual hight and got a $5.00 bill which had been pinned at the top. It is said this parade was halted on Elm street long enough for the removal of the great bronze eagle fastened at the apex of the canopy which covered the float the "Goddess of Liberty" road in, so the procession could pass under the overhead bridge of W. W. Wallace's machine shop. The "Goddess of Liberty" was Miss Elizabeth Bell.

A. C. Bell

This year Greenamyer & Callahan started in the hardware business in the building on the northeast corner of Main and Friend streets.

1877

Valley Forge Machine Shop.

The Valley Forge Machine shops were built in 1877 by Adam Aaron and Sylvester Harrold (three brothers), for general repair work. The shop was run under the firm name of A. Harrold and Bros. In 1879 the works were enlarged and continued under the firm name of J. Harrold and Sons, who manufactured stationary engines. They employed eight men. A few years later, in 1879, the Valley Forge Machine shops were shut down indefinitely.

David slotter opened a Book and Stationery store in a room just west of John Beard's tin store in 1877.

General Ephraim S. Holloway, son of John and Lydia (Dixon) Holloway, was born in Fairfield township, Columbiana County, Ohio, July 27, 1833. Until 1861 he followed the trade of carpenter. In 1861 he enlisted in Company F, Forty-first Regiment, O. V. I., as a private.

During four and a quarter years of service of constant duty with his company and regiment he was advanced and advanced again until he received the rank of Colonel E. S. Holloway and was recommended for promotion to the rank of Brigadier-general of Volunteers by Brevet.

March 1, 1868, he was appointed as superintendent of the Enterprise Agricultural works, which he held until September, 1873.

In November, 1871, he purchased a half interest in the Independent Register office, and besides his other labors he took editorial charge of the paper. In June following he purchased the interest of his partner, Mr. N. E. Nold, and took entire control.

In 1873 Hon. E. S. Holloway was elected representative in the State Legislature and re-elected in 1875 to the sixty-first and sixty-second General Assemblies.

In April, 1877, he was admitted to the bar in Columbus, Ohio, and commenced the practice of law in Columbiana November 1, 1877.

In 1877 W. W. Wallace's manufacturing establishment, the overhead bridge to foundry, paint shop, enameling room, and office, with separate buildings, were totally destroyed by fire.

Joseph Conley opened up a drug store and embarked in the sale of drugs. This store was continued until 1879.

1878

In 1878 O. N. and Fred Gaylord, two brothers, bought the store stock of John Sturgeon and embarked in the drygoods business, under the firm name of Gaylord & Gaylord. They remained but a few years. They removed their stock to a cross-roads storeroom near Ravenna, where they continued the business for many years.

J. B. Williams, a maker of boots and shoes, located, in July, in an upstairs room of the southeast corner of Main street and the public square.

Geo. Esterly and J. M. Williams embarked in the tailoring business under the firm name of Esterly & Williams.

1879

In 1879 George Strickler and John Patterson bought the Reuben Strickler store and continued the business a while under the firm name of Patterson & Strickler.

This year Joseph Conley accepted Dr. A. L. King as partner in his drug store. This store was run under the firm name of Conley & King until 1881.

Reuben Strickler started in the business of selling farm implements and machinery. This business he opened up in a building on a lot on Main street now owned by Mr. J. J. Henry Schlagg, and continued until 1884.

Tidd's Bargain House occupies the large brick block now in course of completion on the northwest corner of Main street and Spring valley. This store will be the largest and most complete Department store in Eastern Ohio. In 1879 S. W. Tidd began in the jewelry business in the Frason block with a ninety dollar stock. In 1889 the Tidd's Racket store was opened up in the Farrand block by Mrs. C. L. Tidd. In May, 1891, for want of more room, the Tidd's Bargain House was moved to the Frason block. In May, 1901, they again moved, this time to the larger rooms in the Deemer building, and in 1905 to their own building on the corner of Main street and Spring alley. Last year work was commenced erecting their new block, which will be completed this fall.

1880

In February, 1880, A. C. Bell became the P., F. W. & C. R. R. agent at Columbiana. During the month of May, Rev. Shillinger taught German in room No. 2 of the school building. This year H. H. Smith opened a general store in the building on the northeast corner of East Park avenue and the public square.

1881

In 1881 Chas. E. Ink purchased Dr. A. L. King's interest in the drug store and Mr. Ink and Mr. Conley continued the business under the firm name of Ink and Conley. A year or two later Mr. Conley sold his interest in the stor to Mr. Ink and left town.

1882

In 1882 the Columbiana Pump and Machine Co. was located on the south side of the east end of Railroad street and was commenced by Daniel and George Strickler in a small shop on the site of the present Columbiana Pump company's works. They continued the business until 1887, when a stock company was formed, with Chars. Frederick, president; Aaron Esterly, secretary; Henry Wining, shop foreman; Robert Martin, foundry foreman; Daniel Strickler, chief pattern maker.

A literary society met in the school hall in 1882 and 1883.

1884

The banking firm of Shilling & Co., composed of S. S. Shilling, Mrs. Caroline Deemer, and David Strohaker, opened up its bank in the Dr. A. L. King office building about May 1, 1884. In 1889 a two-story brick edifice was built on the east side of Main street on the Mrs. Caroline Deeme's property, into which they soon moved. The bank was successful until 1896, when, at the failure of the Columbiana Handle works, Mr. Shilling tried to bridge the financial chasm and put the works on its feet, as it were. The final collapse of the enterprise gradually dragged the banking firm of Shilling & Co. down in the ruin. The depositors received 20 per cent. in the settlement.

This year David S. DeVere opened and fitted up a dyeing factory on North Main street. Mr. DeVere, together with Mr. J. A. French of Springfield, Ohio, and Mr. E. Compton of Pittsburg, Pa., practical workmen in fine chemical dyeing, spent considerable time and money to make their Columbiana factory a success, but after a few months experimenting they abandoned work at this point.

1885

In 1885, Simon Harrold, Amos Harrold, Elmer Harrold and Jacob Detwiler bought the I. Harrold and Sons Machine shops, which were then continued under the firm name of The Enterprise Mfg. Co. They began the manufacturing of saw mills and engines. At this time the floor space was about 35 feet square, with a foundry in connection of about 35x60 feet floor space. In 1890 Elmer Harrold withdrew from the firm, leaving Simon and Amos Harrold, and Jacob Detwiler, to continue the business. In 1894 the sales of their manufactured products had so increased that they were compelled to build a more

commodious shop. In order to do so, land was purchased on the southwest corner of Fairfield avenue and the P., F. W. & C. railroad. On this site a brick structure was erected with floor space of about 60x180 feet. The shop in the hollow was then moved to this location. In 1889 Amos Harrold withdrew from the firm, leaving Jacob Detwiler and the heirs of Simon Harrold to continue the business. In 1908 they were again compelled to enlarge the factory, and now the extensive manufacturing plant occupies the entire block between Main and Elm streets, and almost the same distance south from the P., F. W. & C. railroad tracks. The floor space of The Enterprise Manufacturing Co. shops now is about 50,000 square feet, while 60 to 100 men are employed. Horse road rollers, portable and stationary engines, sawmills and sawmill machinery are manufactured, with an ever increasing demand for their supply.

Free Street Fair

The first street fair was held in Columbiana September 19, 1885. The association officers were as follows: President, A. C. Bell; Vice-President, J. W. Detwiler; Secretary, E. S. Holloway; Treasurer, Bertram Renkenberger. A grand parade was called at 1 P. M., when the stock exhibition joined in under the direction of the marshal of the day and his assistants. Annual free street fairs have been held September 25, 1886; October 1, 1887, and every year since, with the exception of a few times, when omission was caused by lack of interest. The twenty-seventh annual free street fair and home coming was held September 20 and 21, 1912. The association officers are: President, Isaiah Flickinger; Vice-President, R. H. Vaughn; Secretary, S. S. Weaver; Treasurer, N. M. Fuhrman; Executive Committee, J. W. Weaver, I. S. Rauch, Chas. E. Smith, J. R. Jeffreys, H. O. Newell; Entertainment Committee, Chas E. Smith, Mayor Bookwalter, H. A. Inman and H. E. Garrett. The fair this year was arranged to continue two days, and was known as Columbiana's Street Fair and Gala Days.

1886

In 1886 J. Scott White opened a coal yard on the north side of the railroad west of the depot.

1887

D. M. McGaffick sold pumps in this locality during 1887-88-89.

1888

In 1888 a Bell telephone was placed in the Patterson House. For two years this pay station remained in this building. In 1890 it was moved to John E. Allen's drug store. In 1892 was run as an exchange with twenty-five subscribers. In April, 1902, the office was moved into the First National Bank building in the middle room on the second floor facing Main street. The office still remains in this room in the Union Banking Co.'s building. Miss Nora Havil is chief operator.

The Columbiana Handle Co. was organized January 4, 1888 by a stock company. The original plant was started, as the Leetonia Handle Co., by John Oehrle, and operated in the old carding mill between Columbiana and Leetonia, Ohio.

1890

April 15, 1890, Chapter No. 2415 of the Epworth League of the M. E. church of Columbiana was organized by representatives of the Cleveland chapter. The present officers are: President, Hazel Zeiger; First Vice-President, Mary Buzard; Second Vice-President, Mattie Derringer; Third Vice-President, Mae Fry; Fourth Vice-President, Pearl Early; Secretary, Allen Heston; Treasurer, Walter Rupert; Junior League Supterintendent, Elizabeth Flickinger; Organist, Ethel Todd. At present the league has sixty-five members.

Secret Societies—K. of P.

Knights of Pythias of Columbiana was organized August 13, 1890, with twenty members and the following officers: P. C., S. W. Tidd; C. C., J. W. Knaub; V. C., W. H. Hayden; Prelate, T. C. Roach; M. Ex., W. G. Strickler; M. F., J. F. Deemer; K. R. S., R. D. Flickinger; W. A., W. J. Weaver; I. G. Samuel Wetzel; O. G., G. H. Anderson; Trustees, James J. Fetzer, Chas. D. Strickler, Samuel Buffinger. Regular monthly meetings are held Thursday night of each week at 7 o'clock.

Present officers of the lodge are as follows: M. W., Wm. Gilbert; C. C., Clyde Kellog; V. C., Frank Keyser; Prelate, Geo. Holloway; K. R. S., G. Ed. Buzard; M. F., J. L. Hum; M. E., E. E. Sitler; M. A., A. L. McBride; I. G.,

Chas. Fuhrman; O. G., Harvey Rapp; Trustees, Fred Gilbert, Perry Miller, Ralph Sponseller. The nodge now has 96 members.

In 1890 Park Warner opened a shoe store in the Sprinkle block, on the southeast corner of Main street and the public square. This corner is now owned by Emmet S. Coblentz. This store existed about two years and a half.

1891

Isaiah Flickinger started in the sale of fine granite and marble tombstones in 1891. He also bought and sold the Berea flag stones for walks.

The N. M. Fuhrman's Carriage Works, which was in operation on North Main street, at the corporation limits about 1880, was moved to the Railroad street location in '91-'92. This establishment was composed of one three-story building, 100 feet by 40 feet. On the ground floor was the smithing department, while above was the wood-work and trimming departments. In another three-story building, 240 feet by 35 feet, was the finishing and erecting department with a commodious office on Railroad street. It was the largest individual carriage works in the State of Ohio. Almost five years these works have remained idle owing to the advance of the automobile industry, and in June, 1812, the buildings were bought by L. M. Kays, who had them removed.

1892

Mr. George Douglass, a railroad watchman, was placed at the Elm street crossing on the P. F. W. & C. R. R. March 7th, 1892. The watchmen that have kept this crossing since are: James Nolan, Si Metz, Jerry Brick, Gilbert Dennis. The present watchman is Peter Destafano.

1894

November 10th, W. L. Augustine purchased the book and stationary store of David Slotter and continued the business at the same old stand. After the fire in 1907 Mr. Augustine built a fine brick block on the old site and continued his store with a brand new stock.

August 24th, 1894, barns burned by straw being ignited in one of the barns when a lantern was overturned by the kicking of a cow. These barns were built at the back of the different town lots situated on Walnut alley, just south of Pittsburg street, and east of Main street.

March 28th, 1894, Coxey's great "Commonweal" army reached this place on its way to Washington, D. C. The army numbered 150 men. They marched to the Johnston Iron Works, which was named camp Trenton, in honor of the Revolutionary battle-field, where the hoboes were fed. A large crowd listened to speeches by Coxey, the president of the Good Roads Association; Carl Browne; the great unknown, and S. C. Thayer. The recruits from here numbered twenty-five.

1895

In 1895 the Water Works and Electric Light Plant was completed. The town rwas bonded for $38,000 for the purpose. On November 30th, at 7 P. M., Mayor A. C. Bell pushed the button that supplied light to thirty-eight arc lamps suspended over the different streets. The Alcyone Club, an institution, was organized March 1st for the purpose of supplying a reading room and lounging parlors for the young men of our city, who otherwise find time dragging unrelentlessly on their hands. It lasted two years and disbanded. March 20th this same year Mr. J. H. Watt of Pittsburg, Pa., purchased Frederick and Sons' shoe store.

Work was begun on separate fruit houses. Mr. Lower's fruit house, which was sold recently to the Banner Machine Company, is located on Railroad street, and is built of tile blocks. Mr. Entrikin's is a frame and was erected on his lot just west of Main street, on the north side of Strawberry alley.

Water Works and Electric Light Plant

June 18th gates were first installed on the Main street crossing of the P. F. W. & C. R. R., with John Holsapfel as gateman.

March 4th G. G. Chamberlain and H. H. Snapp purchased the stock of groceries formerly owned by Noah Strickler, and under the firm name of Snapp & Chamberlain opened up a grocery store in the Frederick block.

July 28th Miss Ella Hahn of Canton organized a Woman's Foreign Missionary Society in the M. E. church. The following officers were elected:

President, Mrs. J. T. Morton; first vice-president, Mrs. W. R. Butcher; second vice-president, Mrs. George Bare; third vice-president, Mrs. A. Overholt; corresponding secretary, Mrs. D. S. DeVere; recording secretary, Miss Mattie Turkle; treasurer, Mrs. M. A. Todd.

Monthly meetings are held regularly ever since August 1st, this year.

July 11th Martin Griffith, of Irondale, purchased the E. L. Roninger furniture store and took possession a few days later.

September 1st Dr. W. D. Holloway, who had his dental parlors in the Beatty block on Main street, removed to Philadelphia, Pa.

John R. and William Jeffreys succeeded J. H. Watt, shoe dealer, September 18th. They continued the business under the firm name of Jeffrey's Bros.

Jacob Yoder opened a feed store on Friend street and dealt in building material also.

January, 1895, the Columbiana Boiler Works was established by Amos Harrold, Simon Harrold, Jacob Detwiler and John Barrow. The first intention was to make boilers for the Enterprise Mfg. Co.'s use in constructing their steam road rollers and traction engines alone, but soon other work began to come in. They were compelled to increase the size of the shop and employ more men until at one time they employed 80 men. In March, 1900, the Columbiana Boiler Works was incorporated under the laws of the State at Columbus, Ohio, by Simon Harrold, Chas. I. Harrold, Jacob Detwiler, Edwin Detwiler,

COLUMBIANA, OHIO. Manufacturing Plants

John Barrow. This shop now manufactures boilers and all other classes of iron plate work. The officers for 1911-'12 are: Jacob Detwiler, president; Chas. I. Harrold, vice-president; Mrs. L. Harrold, Mrs. J. J. Fetzer; John Barrow, treasurer and general manager.

In 1895 Curtis Stahl began dealing in coal in cahload lots. He now operates a large coal yard on East Park avenue, along the Y. & S. trolley line.

1896

April 6th, 1896, the first water works and electric light trustees were elected. The names of the newly-elected trustees are as follows: E. J. Wolfgang, president; W. T. Holloway, secretary; Frank Bell, superintendent.

July 27th the Cola. Board of Trade was organized with the following named officers for the ensuing year:

President, N. M. Fuhrman; first vice-president, T. J. Mason; second vice-president, W. R. Knowles; secretary, H. O. Newell; treasurer, J. G. Beatty.

The following were elected directors, who with the officers constitute the Board of Directors: C. E. Ink, A. Greenamyer, J. A. Linville, Amos Harrold, Solomon Culp, H. G. Bye, Chas. Frederick, Enos Zeigler, W. T. Holloway, A. C. Bell.

March 1st J. N. Yoder embarked in the tile and brick business combined with the sales of various other building materials.

J. Esterly & Company for many years did the leading banking business in our little city. In 1896 Mr. J. Esterly, the president of the company, died. December 1st the J. Esterly & Company bank went into litigation. The receiver settled up the affairs in 1904, the creditors receiving 33 per cent.

1897

During the financial stringency in the spring of 1897 an organization was inaugurated in the J. B. Caughey veterinary surgeon's office, which was located on his property on the southwest corner of Elm street and Strawberry alley, with about thirty members. The organization was called "The Labor Exchange." The members could bring buggies, wagons, horses and anything like quantities of brooms, etc., manufactured by themselves, for the organization, and they would be exchanged with any of the similar associations or exchanges, which then existed throughout the United States. They issued script money in fractionable units with which they paid bills. The Columbiana branch existed about one year. The officers were as follows: President, J. J. Harrold; secretary, J. B. Caughey; manager, Jacob Zimmer; accountant, Samuel Zellars. At one time an exchange was accomplished with a similar organization in St. Louis, Mo.

April 5th H. C. Welch, of New Brighton, Pa., opened up a hotel business in the Patterson House. He remained only a few weeks.

May 25th David E. Candel opened a furniture store in the Frederick block.

Harry Todd accepted the position of baggage agent at the P. F. W. & C. R. R. depot, which was then left vacant by the withdrawal of Mr. Candel.

November 1st Irvin Rauch, of Leetonia, purchased a half interest in Peter Frason's boot and shoe store, located in the building where Crawford's grocery store is now. The business was continued until Mr. Frason's death under the firm name of Frason & Rauch. Mr. Rauch then bought Mr. Frason's interest and continued the business under the name of I. S. Rauch Shoe Store.

M. C. Harrison and T. E. Long, of Pittsburg, Pa., purchased the Columbiana Pump & Machine Co.'s plant and started the wheels moving Friday, August 23rd, '97. Henry Wining is still foreman of the machine shop. The business was carried on under the firm name of The Columbiana Pump Co.

1898

Secret Societies—K. O. T. M. of the World.

K. O. T. M. of the World was organized at Columbiana October 17th, 1898, with fourteen members and the following officers: Adin Greenamyer, P. Sr. Kt. Com.; Isaiah Flickinger, Sir Kt. Com.; S. H. Kurtz, Sir Kt. Lt. Com.; D. E. Candel, Sir Kt. R. K.; W. J. Flickinger, Sir Kt. E. K.; John Beck, Sir Kt. Chaplain; A. S. H. Johnson, Sir Kt. of Sergt.; W. T. Whan, Sir Kt. of Phy.; J. J. Johnson, Sir Kt. Mat. A.; R. E. Pritchard, Sir Kt. 1st M. O. of G.; C. A. Inman, Sir Kt. 2nd M. O. of G.

Regular monthly meetings are held.

The lodge today has thirteen members, with the following officers: Wm. Lemley, P. Com.; Cyrus Chamberlain, Commander; Harvey Harrold, Lt. Com.; O. O. Glosser, R. K.; John Zimmer, Chaplain.

In 1898 Snapp & Son embarked in the grocery business. This store existed two years. This year D. E. Candel & Co. opened up a furniture store in the Frederick block. This block burned down in 1900, when Mr. Candel quit the business.

April 1st, 1898, Wm. Culp and Rob't Martin formed a partnership in the blacksmith business on East Park avenue, near the Public Square. They dissolved May 31st, just two months later.

1899

Dr. John J. Looney located here about May 1st, 1899, in the northeast corner building on Main and Friend streets. He practiced medicine actively until his death a few years later.

In 1899 Ike Handlesman ran a gent's clothing house next door to the bank.

The Columbiana County Independent Telephone Co., a new company just incorporated at Columbus, under the laws of the state, began erecting poles in Columbiana county. The first telephone pole to be placed by them was the one on the corner of Main and Friend streets, June 25th, this year.

Chris Kuegle purchased J. G. Green's furniture store January 24th. Mr. Green had been in business about three years.

January 30th fire occurred in the 250 foot section of N. M. Fuhrman's Carriage Works. The loss was estimated at from $8,000 to $10,000.

1900

A. C. Yengling, commander, and nineteen members of Trescott Post, G. A. R., of Salem, assisted in re-mustering the James A. Garfield Post in Columbiana. The following officers were installed: P. C., Peter Bushong; J. V. C., J. D. Holloway; S. M., John G. Beatty; S. V. C., Joseph Hisey; O. of D., H. C. Early; O. of G., David Havil; Surgeon, John A. Todd; Adjutant, Thomas Candel; Chaplain, J. I. Sample. Regular meetings have been held in their rooms ever since.

On March 19th curfew began.

Milo S. Rau and C. Fred Staley purchased the Snapp & Son's grocery and began business under the firm name of Rau & Staley in the Frederick block April 1st, 1900.

1901

The Columbiana Pump Company

In 1900 M. C. Harrison sold his interest in the Columbiana Pump Co. to J. V. Stewart, who, with T. E. Long, continued the business of the Columbiana

Pump Co. In 1907 they erected a fine brick foundry. This foundry is 80 feet by 100 feet in dimensions. In 1910 they erected a brick "L" shaped machine shop, which is a two-story, 50x200-foot building with basement. This entire shop is warmed in winter by heater, and machinery has gas engine drive. They manufacture iron and brass pumps, cylinder hydrants, and hydraulic rams. Their shipments are large; some days they are known to have shipped several carloads of their product to the markets. Fifty men are employed Robert Martin is foundry foreman, while Henry Wining has charge of the entire works.

In 1901, after learning the trade of machine blacksmith at the Enterprise Mfg. Co.'s shops, Harvey Harrold formed a partnership with William Culp and began the business of horse-shoer and blacksmith on the corner of Middle and Lisbon streets. Harrold and Culp run a very successful shop as geneeral blacksmiths. In 1909 Mr. Harrold discovered a process to harden and toughen steel, and entered into tool manufacturing on a very small scale. 1910 he was compelled on account of increase of business to install heavy machinery, such as trip hammers and furnaces. Floor space was necessary and he was compelled to build and move into larger quarters. His shops are located on his property on the northeast corner of West Park avenue and Walnut alley, just west of the Public Square, where he manufactures all kinds of hand tools and does general forging.

On February 2nd the H. H. Smith & Sons Co. was incorporated at Columbiana, Ohio. The company was composed of H. H. Smith and his four sons, viz.: Chas. E., Wm. B., Geo. A., and H. Edgar. They owned a department store on the southwest corner of Main street and the public square. Mr. H. H. Smith died July 7, 1909. In order to close up the estate the children proceeded to sell out. July 11, 1911, J. H. Tope and J. A. Crawford bought the grocery department. They took possession August 1, 1911, and under the rm name of Tope & Crawford they opened their store on the west side of Main street, two doors south of Mulberry alley. November 15, 1911, Mr. Tope sold his interest in the store to Mr. Crawford, who still continues the business under the business name of J. A. Crawford. December 11, 1911, they sold their dry goods store to F. D. Lodge, who took possession January 1, 1912. The cloth-

H. H. Smith

goods store to F. D. Lodge, who took possession January 1st, 1912. The clothing department was closed out entirely and on March, 1912, Chas. E. Smith opened up for sale an entire new line of gent's furnishings in his own storeroom on the east side of Main street, next door south of the postoffice. The H. H. Smith estate is slowly being closed up.

March, 1901, W. H. Baker and J. C. Harrold dissolved partnership in the blacksmithing trade.

On March 19th the Columbiana Lumber Co. dissolved partnership. The members of this company were as follows: Chas. Holloway, J. B. Ziegler, C. S. Lehman and C. V. Calvin.

April 6th D. A. Heck, clothier, closed up his line of business by auction.

On April 20th A. Bobenrieth sold his china store, which he run in connection with his laundry, at public auction, and closed up his business.

April 1st J. B. Fitzpatrick opened up a full line of buggies, surries, phaetons and driving wagons in the Thomas building on the east side of Main street, north of Railroad street.

The snow storm April 20th and 21st was the worst ever experienced this time of the year in Columbiana. The snow began Friday morning and fell continuously until late Saturday morning. Between twenty inches to two feet was measured on the level.

S. S. Stewart located here September, 1901, and started a drug store. This store was sold to Mr. H. B. Law when Mr. Stewart became postmaster.

1902

February 1st, 1902, was the inauguration of the rural free delivery of mail in Columbiana. Isaac Culp, James Mather, A. S. H. Johnson were installed as carriers No. 1, No. 2, No. 3. Mr. Johnson died September 30th, 1909, when John B. Sitler, who acted as substitute, became carrier No. 3. In April, 1912, James Mather resigned and May 19th, 1912, Selby Hull was installed as carrier No. 2.

E. J. Wolfgang

On June 5th, 1902, E. J. Wolfgang, a civil engineer, of Columbiana, and a crew of three men, accompanied by the promoters of the venture, John H. Ruhlman, Asa Jones and the Long brothers, began the preliminary survey of the prospective course of the Youngstown & Southern Railway. The profile drafting was finished with great care and accuracy, and met the promoters' most sanguine expectations. The final route at last accepted followed his survey with but few variations. Mr. Wolfgang in 1878 opened up the first gun and sewing machine repair shop in Columbiana in Joel Moreland's building, located on the southwest corner of Main street and Spring alley. He located here in 1860, coming from his father's home in Maryland, and soon after began the milling business in the Mr. John Nold grist mill, about two miles and a half west of town.

April 5th, this year, Rau & Staley sold their grocery store to Weller & Mowen Bros., who continued the business at the old stand in the Frederick block. They were burnt out February 7th, 1904, but they started up again March 18th, '04. February, 1908, they sold their store to Mrs. L. E. Reck.

The origin of the present Youngstown & Southern Railway is due to the good management of John H. Ruhlman, Asa Jones, the Long brothers and other Youngstown parties interested in the project. In June, 1902, E. J. Wolfgang, a civil engineer, began a preliminary survey of the prospective course of this road. The road was completed in 1904. A bill announcing the opening of the Columbiana end of the road reads as follows: "Opening of the Youngstown & Southern Railroad. To celebrate the arrival of the first train over the Youngstown & Southern Railway, the business men of Columbiana have engaged Thoman's Concert Band to give a concert at the Columbiana end of the line and then go by train to Ruhlman's Grove, where they will play all day, Saturday, October 8, 1904. Train leaves Park avenue at 9 A. M., 11 A. M., 2 P. M., 5 P. M., 8 P. M., last train returning at midnight."

For some time No. 42, a steam engine, was used as motive power. April 29th, 1907, the first car was run from Youngstown to Leetonia by electricity. Mr. E. S. Flickinger is ticket agent. Mr. A. N. Tannihill is night agent. The sub-station, which had been located at North Lima, is now located in the south room of the depot at this place.

July 2nd, 1902, the First National Bank opened up in what was known as the Esterly & Co. bank building, but now where H. A. Keller's hardware store is located. John E. Allen was its first president, and N. M. Bassinger, cashier;

the directors were as follows: C. M. Schmick, W. Harry Schmick, G. Ed. Buzard, J. E. Allen, Jacob Detwiler, J. V. Stewart and N. M. Bassinger. They bought a site for building the same year and erected a three-story brick edifice, which they occupied about April, 1904. On December 15, 1909, they voluntarily liquidated their affairs and sold to the Union Banking Co.

Tidd & Harman formed a partnership in the jewelry business October 15th. They dissolved partnership September 1st, 1912.

The W. C. T. U.

The Woman's Christian Temperance Union was organized in the Disciple church July, 1904, with twenty-four charter members, by Jeannette Fuller, a State organizer and lecturer, of Austinburg, Ohio, assisted by Mrs. Mary Cope, Mrs. Jean G. Curry and Miss Ida K. Curry. The first officers were as follows: President, Miss Ida K. Curry; corresponding secretary, Mrs. Leora Koch; recording secretary, Miss Dora B. Inman; treasurer, Mrs. J. F. Kirkbride. A banquet and an annual election was held in the Duquesne Manfg. Co.'s building August 16th, 1912. A new office had been created, and the present officers are as follows: President, Mrs. I. S. Rauch; vice-president at large, Miss Ida K. Curry; corresponding secretary, Mrs. Blanche Boyer; recording secretary, Mrs. Clara T. Moore; treasurer, Miss Edna Vankirk. There are 118 present members.

1904

In 1904 F. C. and C. A. Hartman, two brothers, began the manufacture of their celebrated Hartman Tobies in a room in the Frederick block. They left town in September, 1906. Other cigar makers plied their trades at this place at different times. This year Jesse Green, Jr., a dealer in all kinds of thoroughbred poultry, pheasants, fancy game, water fowls and ornamental birds, conducted his salesrooms at his home on his chicken farm on Cross street. Mr. Green furnished a number of State Game Commissioners with game-birds for propagation on State game farms. His many sales caused numerous importations of very scarce varieties of pheasants and black swans from Germany. The Ohio Pheasantry was run until 1910.

In 1904, after Theodore Koch moved his grocery store from the corner rooms on the northwest corner of Main and Railroad streets, where Ira Smith

had occupied for a number of years, to his rooms in the Frederick block, Royal Conkey was in the hardware business for about two years in these rooms.

Harvey Rapp built a machine shop on this lot east of Main street and north of Duquesne street, in October, 1904, and attends to the plumbing work in town. A plumbing shop was opened in the Frederick block about seven years ago by Brentzel & Swanson. This shop was run for about two years. J. J. Johnston also opened and operated a plumbing establishment in a room on the east side of Main street and south of the Public Square for a few years.

1905

Columbiana's Centennial was celebrated August 21, 1905, by the H. H. Smith So's Co.ns annual pumpkin show, which always drew a large crowd. Hon. Charles S. Speaker, of Lisbon, Ohio, the county seat of Columbiana county, made an address on the early history of Columbiana and Fairfield township to about 9,000 people. The entertainment of the day consisted in wheel-barrow, potato, egg and girl races and a ball game was played on the home grounds between the Hazelton and Columbiana teams.

1906

The Columbiana Handle Co. was operated as a stock company until March, 1906, at which time Shilling & Co.'s bank failed, and the stockholders in order to protect themselves made an assignment and appointed T. A. Renkenberger receiver, who operated until August 24th, 1906, when it was sold at receiver's sale to the present owneis, F. H. Grove, C. V. Calvin and T. A. Renkenberger, who operated for two years and then incorporated under the laws of the State of Ohio by the name of the Columbiana Mfg. Co. The present officers of the company are: F. H. Grove, president; C. V. Calvin, secretary; T. A. Renkenberger, treasurer and general manager.

The present company have added several buildings and three acres of ground and aie engaged in the manufacturing of all kinds of tool handles, ornamental concrete work and planing mill work.

In 1906 W. O. Wallace, attorney-at-law, of East Palestine, Ohio, located here and began the practice of his profession November 1st.

May 10th the Columbiana Bank & Savings Co. began business in the southeast corner room of the Frederick block on the northwest corner of Main and Union streets. The first president was J. R. Jeffries; vice-president, C. S. Lehman, and cashier, E. P. Funkhouser. The Board of Directors were as follows: J. R. Jeffries, C. S. Lehman, John W. Detwiler, S. A. Randon, W. J. Caldwell, Ira Seachrist, Royal Conkey, J. J. Quigley, D. R. Lehman, S. E. Houk, S. J. Heck, Isaiah Flickinger, I. T. Rohrer, M. H. Stooksberry and Harry Bookwalter. December 15th, 1909, they voluntarily liquidated their affairs and sold to the Union Banking Co.

1907

About the first of September, 1907, the Columbiana Foundry Co. erected a fine new brick building on their land which lies between the P. F. W. & C. R. R. tracks and the Y. & S. trolley line in the southern part of the town, west of Main street. This foundry is owned by the Wm. Tod Co., of Youngstown, and turns out the small castings that that company requires. The foundry gives steady employment to thirty men.

1908

April, 1908, The Duquesne Manufacturing Co. was established by the Pittsburg Drygoods Co. They located in a building erected by the Board of Trade of Columbiana, on Railroad street, opposite the P., F. W. & C. R. R. depot. Part of this building was the former David Scott hotel. It is a two-story brick structure, 50 feet wide and 163 feet deep, and was built according to the various needs of the company. A forty horse-power gas engine supplies power for the operation of 200 sewing machines, in a long well-ventilated and well-lighted room on the second floor; a large dynamo on the first floor supplies light on dark days and when needed for overtime work, as well as the improved electric cutting knife which Mr. Shinn so deftly operates. Mr. R. S. Breckenridge is manager of the plant. W. E. Shinn is in charge of the cutting department. Mrs. R. A. Zeigler is the efficient forelady in the sewing room, and Ray Culp is the shipping clerk.

The company manufactures men's shirts, blouses, and overalls, and women's aprons, wrappers, shirtwaists, and petticoats.

All of the completed garments are at once boxed and shipped to the Pittsburg Dry Goods Co., Pittsburg, Pa.

November 15 J. J. Fesler bought the grocery store of Mrs. L. E. Reck and continued the business in the same room, in the Beatty block, on Main street.

On October 8 the Wells Fargo Express Co. began business at the different towns along the Y. & S. trolley lines, with E. S. Flickinger as its first agent at this point.

1909

January 1st, 1909, Wm. Lauten built a small brass foundry on his lot on the east side of South Main street. In this foundry for about a year all of the brass mouldings for the Enterprise Mfg. Co. were turned out.

March 1st Harry Owens began business in dry cleaning men's clothing. He was one of the firm of Agnew & Co., who carried on that department of the Agnew's tailoring establishment for about two weeks.

Dr. R. D. Morford and Edward Jackson rented the Krohmer House, the hotel on the southwest corner lot of Main street and the railroad, and opened up the hotel to the needs of the general public. The name of this hotel was "Hotel Jackson." It had an existence of about two years.

December 15, 1909, the Union Banking Co. began business by purchasing the assets and good will of the First National Bank and the Columbiana Bank & Savings Co. The first Board of Directors to represent the new bank were: Jacob Detwiler, John E. Allen, D. R. Lehman, G. Ed. Buzard, Jerry Shontz, J. V. Stewart, J. J. Quigley, S. W. Tidd, J. A. Vogleson, Harry Bookwalter, Royal Conkey and J. R. Jeffries. The first officers were chosen as follows: President, J. V. Stewart; vice-president, J. R. Jeffries; cashier, E. P. Funkhouser; assistant cashier, V. C. Bassinger; secretary, J. W. Weaver.

Hallowe'en Carnival.

Mrs. J. M. Webb suggested the first Hallowe'en Carnival, which was held in Columbiana in 1909. It was an enjoyable event and similar occasions have been observed annually ever since with growing interest.

The Banner Machine Company was organized November, 1909, for the manufacture of vacuum cleaners and small specialties by C. D. Rymer, F. H. Grove, C. M. Hoover, H. H. Hoover, R. H. Grove and S. W. Seidner. The manufacture of the Ohio Oil Cloth Rack is their main specialty. Their shop is located on the south side of Railroad street, just east of the Boiler Works.

The Banner Machine Co. is incorporated under the laws of the State of Ohio with the following officers: C. D. Rymer, president; H. M. Hoover, vice-president; F. H. Grove, secretary; C. M. Hoover, treasurer; R. H. Grove, manager.

Sunset Temple, No. 364, Pythian Sisters, was instituted April 21st, 1909, in the K. of P. Hall by Francis Hardman, of Cleveland, O., assisted by the members of Lisbon Temple, with thirty-four charter members. The officers were as follows: M. E. C., Mary Buzard; E. S., Anna Zellars; E. J., Omah Miller; Man., Emma Lewis; M. of R. and C., Mabel Wining; M. of F., Nellie Renkenberger; Pro., Bessie Culp; Guard, Myrtle Konkle; P. C., Amelia Haag; trustees, Della Stahl, Lizzie Wining and Gay Sponseller; captain of staff, Adaline Caldwell.

The present officers are: M. E. C., Mary Sitler; E. S., Lizzie Wining; E. J., Grace Keyser; Man., Nannie Keyser; M. of R. and C., Mary Buzard; M. of F., Iona Flickinger; Pro., Salinda Holloway; Guard, Nina Crawford; P. C.,

Mary Hannum; Trustees, Mary Troll, Myrtle Konkle and Metta Lyons; captain of staff, Myrtle Konkle; installing officer, Mary Buzard. Number of present members is forty-five.

1910

March 4th, 1910, John Ryan opened up a Racket Store in the room on the southwest corner of Main street and the Public Square. After the fire, which destroyed the block May 1st, 1911, he sold out and quit the business.

1911

January 1st, 1911, the Men's Personal Work League of Columbiana was organized. This happened to be on the first day of the week, the first day of the month and the first day of the year. The purpose of the organization is to bring men to the personal knowledge and saving power of our Lord Jesus Christ. The meeting was called to order and S. E. Rogers was elected its president; J. R. Jeffries, vice-president; J. S. White, secretary; Jacob Detwiler, treasurer, and S. S. Weaver, chorister. After the organization seventy-two charter members signed the paper circulated among them for that purpose. The league grew very rapidly until it became a power for good, and many were added to the churches and Sabbath schools. The present membership is 286.

In 1911 Frank Snauffer and Jacob Hum bought the S. S. Wetzel's slating establishment on Main street and continued the business at the same old stand east of Union street.

On February 14th, 1911, the Hattie Bishop Circle was organized with seventy-six charter members. The officers were as follows: President, Mrs. Emma Shenly, Senior V. Pres., Mrs. Henry Koch; Junior V. Pres., Mrs. Mary Hannum; Sec'y, Mrs. Harvey Keller; Treas Mrs. Henry Staley; Guard, Mrs. J. Oberholtzer; Asst. Guard, Mrs. Chas. Strickler; Conductor, Miss Mattie Derringer; Asst. Conductor, Mrs. R. M. Basler; Chaplain, Mrs. J. I. Sample.

This year in March the Beard Stephan Co. located here. They purchased property just west of the corporation limits, lying between the P. F. W. & C. Railroad tracks and the Leetonia road. A shop was erected on these grounds, in which will be manufactured as a specialty Crane Hooks, with an automatic weighing attachment. They intend to soon install an acetyline welding plant for general repair work. By this means they will be able to weld all broken castings, no matter what kind of metal. They are now contracting with another firm to manufacture for said firm an automatic sound machine. By this appliance sailors can ascertain the depth of water at sea on board ship.

October 18th J. R. McDonald started a restaurant next door north of Mrs. F. F. Garrett's millinery store. April 1st he discontinued the restaurant and opened up a pool and billiard room in the J. O. Johnson house at the corner of Main and Railroad streets.

1912

In March, 1912, G. B. Keyser opened up a Racket Store just south of the southwest corner of Main street and the Public Square.

The headquarters of the International Bible Students' Association, commonly called "Millenial Dawn" of Columbiana, is at the home of Cyrus Chamberlain, on Pearl street. Their regular meetings are called "The Weekly Ecclesia." They have about twenty-five members. Annually an "Elder" is chosen to lead the weekly lessons for the ensuing year. The "Millenial Dawn" is known to have had its inception in Columbiana as early as 1876.

On July 20th Ohl Bros. sold their entire line of goods in the building on the southwest corner of Main street and the Public Square at fire sale, and closing out at auction they quit the business.

About 1830 John Young sold a few drugs in a room in his house, which stood where Tidd's Bargain House now stands, then Allen & Co. The druggists who have at different times located here are: Icenhour & Allen, T. C. Allen, Mr. James Stephenson, John E. Allen, Richard Davis, Paul Metzger, Joseph Conley, George Lamb, Chas. Orr, Conley & King, James Todd, Ink & Conley, C. E. Ink, D. K. Uncapher, M. V. Decker, S. S. Stewart. At present Columbiana has three drug stores run by H. B. Law, Ed. Lodge and C. B. Clapp.

The present Adams' Express agent is O. O. Glosser.

A jeweler located in Granny Sturgeon's hotel and repaired clocks and watches as early as 1846. He was here only about a year. A Mr. McMikel, a jeweler, located in Joe Hivel's hotel, which was on a lot on Main street, just south of Mulberry alley, in 1851. E. H. McKee, a watchmaker, was here in 1873. A Mr. Marks was plying his trade for a number of years on Main street. A. Sturgeon made and repaired clocks on the west side of Main street. Other jewelers have located here at different times. Those that are here at present are P. M. Koch and Tidd & Harman.

In 1873 J. T. Barclay, a surgeon dentist, located his dental parlor in a room on the southeast corner of East Park avenue and the Public Square. About this time Robt. Bell opened a dental office in rooms at his home on Fairfield avenue. These are the names of dentists that have been here at different times: Drs. Mason, Dole, T. J. Mason, Jos. Rothwell, J. H. Stooksberry, William Holloway, F. E. Renkenberger, William S. Baker and P. H. Felger.

In 1874 J. G. Augustine was in the harness business in a room on South Main street. Those who also plied their trades here at different times, as can be learned, are as follows:: F. A. Knowles, W. R. Knowles, who is still in business; ──── Railey, Chas. Miller, Bertram Renkenberger, Jesse Elgerton and Frederick Thoman.

John Vogleson began work at the shoemaker's bench in 1831. Daniel Stouffer started in the business in '34. The names of the cobblers that later were in Columbiana are as follows: David Stouffer, Edward Vogleson, John Troll, Solomon Hass, Wm. George, Chas. Stroth, Abe Maneval, Chas. Strabaugh, T. G. Hercher, John Kircher, Lewis Trucksass, Edward Vogan, John Keller, J. J. Johnston, Jeremiah Stall, Nicholas Wining, William Essenwein, Thomas Burgham. The present shoemakers are: Ira Tullis, in the repair department of I. S. Rauch shoe store, and W. S. (Pap) Owens, who is working in the Jeffreys Bros. repair shop at the back of their large and well equipped shoe store, on Main street.

John Stiver, history tells us, was the first contractor worthy of mentioning. He erected the Icenhour residence in 1857, on the southeast corner of Main and Railroad streets. In 1864 the school building on Pittsburg street was completed under his supervision. He also superintended the erection of other buildings. Jacob Detwiler erected in 1883 the north addition to the school house which was completed in 1864. Solomon Culp and Ralph Keller were also local contractors of no small note.

Joseph Wallace was the first recorded commission man. Following are those that came in their turn: John E. Icenhour, Joe Freese, Geo. Kipp, Andrew Lentz, Fred Snauffer, John Snauffer, Andrew Emanuel, William Grove, J. B. Powell, S. F. Hisey, Thomas Entriken, John Vansyckle, Joseph Entriken, J. W. Detwiler, J. O. Entriken and Ferrall & Grimm.

The present commission men are Uriah Shillinger & Son and H. E. Detwiler.

Columbiana's coal dealers are as follows: Frank Vanskivers bought and sold coal in car-load lots about 1878. J. Scott White entered the retailing of coal from his coal yards on Railroad stree in 1886. Curtis Stahl sold coal from his coal yeards in 1895.

Since the P. F. W. & C. R. R. came through and freight accumulated at the depot, the city draymen were as follows: Isaac (Dad) Hill, Ruben Hum, Frank Bell and William C. Hum.

There is no better indication of the prosperity of a town than the postoffice receipts. The annual receipts of Columbiana postoffice have nearly doubled in the past six years.

The money order department receipts amount to less than formerly, but there is a larger amount paid out to local merchants and manufacturers indicating a healthy local trade.

A postal savings bank was opened November 20th, 1911, but owing to the low rate of interest paid it has not proven very popular.

Columbiana Municipal Government

The Village of Columbiana was vested with the privileges of a corporate body in 1837. Under the charter an election for village officers was held at the hotel of John Sturgeon in the Square May 27th, 1837. Emanuel Brubaker and John Snyder acted as judges, and declared the following persons elected: Mayor, William Hickman; Recorder, Samuel Nichols; Trustees, Peter W. DeHoff;, David Neidig, Lot Holmes, William Nichols, Isaac Keister.

Prior to the surrender of the charter in 1842 the following were the mayors: William Hickman, Samuel Seachrist, John C. Young and John Vogleson.

For fourteen years Columbiana was unincorporated, but on the 9th of June, 1856, a new charter was granted, mayors were as follows:

1858—Geo. Lamb. 1859—E. C. Cloud. 1860—Wm. W. Orr. 1861—T. C. Allen. 1862—Geo. Lamb. 1863—Samuel Kyle. 1864—T. C. Allen. 1865—J. D. King. 1866—Geo. O. Frazier. 1867—J. T. Barclay. 1868-1869—T. C. Allen. 1870-1871—Geo. Duncan. 1872-1873—A. C. Yengling. 1874—Josiah Rohrbaugh. 1875—Frank P. Farrand. 1876-1889—A. C. Bell. 1890-1891—John Augustine. 1892-1893—N. M. Fuhrman. 1894-1895—A. C. Bell. 1896-1897—T. J. Mason. 1898-1905—Bertraham Renkenberger (the mayor becoming ill December 1st. 1902—Dayton Fisher, as president of council, served unfilled term. 1905-1909—Samuel Tidd. 1910-1911—J. Ross Flickinger. 1912—Harry Bookwalter.

Hotels

In 1808 Michael Croxen had a primitive hotel (tavern) on the southwest corner of what is now known as West Park avenue and the Public Square. This tavern was later kept by Caleb Roller.

On the corner opposite, north, George Welch kept an inn.

On the corner opposite, east, from Welch's tavern was another, kept by Isaac Williamson.

John Sturgeon kept a tavern where Mr. Dale Stouffer lives. Soon after taking possession and running this hotel but a short time he took Caleb Roller's place on the Public Square. In 1849 Granny Sturgeon took charge until 1865. In 1865 Jacob Greenamyer purchased this property and in 1870 the present "Park House" was erected.

On the southwest corner of Main and Union streets Christopher Hively owned a hotel. This building has passed into the following owners' hands: Scott, Robinson, Ferrall and Vogleson.

David Scott erected a commodious brick building for a hotel on Railroad street opposite the Pennsylvania depot. This hotel was only run for a short time, when it was sold to Dr. Geo. Metzger.

In 1878 the Patterson House was opened by J. P. Patterson, and being centrally located received a good trade from the traveling public. Later Mr. Christopher Smith bought this property. About fifteen years ago Mr. Alex Johnson ran the hotel for about a year.

In the spring of 1890 Mrs. Cathern Troll and daughters, Kate and Sophia, began the hotel business in the Patterson building. They moved soon after to their newly completed home on the east side of Main street, three doors north of the churches, where the Troll sisters continued in the hotel business. This hotel is known as the "Troll House."

A distillery was in operation on a lot just south of Mrs. S. H. Zellars' residence property in Columbiana about 1810. It was owned and operated by Joshua Dixon, the founder of our beautiful village, who afterwards disposed of the property to Wm. Moody. It next passed into the hands of Jeremiah Steltz and Christopher Shirey, along about 1840. Later it was owned by Frederick and Christopher Bonnaberger, but their management was not of the best. Financial troubles soon caused the firm to go into liquidation and the property was sold at sheriff's sale to Dr. Geo. Metzger. Mr. Metzger soon cleared the land by disposing of the buildings to John Fitzpatrick and Dr. Daniel Deemer, respectively.

A tannery was in operation just north of the village and was carried on for a number of years by a Mr.

J. J. Schauweker

McClun. After his death the son, Joseph McClun, carried on the business. He received thirty-five acres and the tannery, as his inheritance. Joseph erected a small brick residence on the land in the forks of the Canfield and North Lima roads. A few years later Mr. McClun sold the tannery to a Mr. Betz. Mr. Betz, becoming discouraged soon after the purchase, sold the tannery to J. J. Schauweker, who for many years was very successful, turning out a line of hand-tanned leather equal to none.

Dams Near Columbiana

These dams furnished power for grist mills and saw mills. They all existed before 1848:

South—John and Benj. Bushong's, on the head waters of Mill Creek.
Southeast—James Caldwell's, on Caldwell's Run.
North—John Crumbacker's, on small branch of Mill Creek.
Northwest—Christopher Hively's, on Mill Creek.
West—Stacy Nichols—Jacob Nold's old dam—on Cherry Fork.
Jacob Nold's (built later and called it the new dam) on Embree's Run.
John Summers, on Cherry Fork, west of Nold's.
Southwest—Moses Embree's, on Embree's Run.
Edward Mann's, on Embree's Run.

Columbiana holds the record of having free delivery of mail before even the city of New York had the system.

John Hiner

John Hiner, whose picture you see above, was one of the first postmasters in the place. He was an eccentric and cranky old fellow, and held the job a number of years. He was so cranky that he did not want people coming to his house for their mail, so he delivered it to them at their homes, saying that he did not want to be bothered handing it to them from his window.

Thus it is that Columbiana holds the banner when it comes to free mail delivery, for she had it almost seventy-five years ago.

Postmasters

Those that have successively filled the position as postmaster at this place are as follows:

John Dixon, Jesse Allen, William Moody, John Young, Wm. Sturgeon, Anthony Hardman, Peter DeHoff, John Hiner, Capt. J. H. Bell, David Esterly, Geo. Lower, Wm. Halverstadt, Bert Renkenberger, Ed. I. Snyder, S. S. Stewart.

Mail Messengers

In the year 1854 when the P. F. W. & C. railroad was a proven and sure mode of travel, the mail, which had been carried overland by the stage route, was henceforth carried by rail, and the stage was abondoned and went into history.

The mail was transferred from the depot at this place to the post-office by a government mail messenger hired for the purpose.

The names of those employed at this work are as follows:
Jonathan Fesler
John Hiner
Jacob Hum
Robert Hoskinson
Ross Flickinger
G. Washington Cole
Nathan Cole
Edward Shillinger
Lee Arnold
Noah Orr
William Basler
Ralph Basler
Lester McGaffick
Chauncey E. Wolfgang

S. S. Stewart

Roster of Soldiers in Rebellion Enlisted from Columbiana

Twenty-Fourth Regiment, Ohio Volunteer Infantry—Company C

Captain David J. Higgins, enlisted June 1, 1861; promoted to colonel January 1, 1863; resigned October 23, 1863.

Captain Wm. C. Beck, enrolled as sergeant, promoted to first sergeant, then second lieutenant, then first lieutenant, then captain, April 21, 1864; mustered out June 22, 1864.

First Sergeant Jno. R. Baker, Fairfield township; died October 7, 1861.

Sergeant Robt. T. Billingsley, Middleton township; died October 4, 1861.

Sergeant Wm. C. Beck, Fairfield township, promoted to captain.

Corporal Israel J. Deemer, Fairfield township; promoted to sergeant.

Corporal Lindley H. Tullis, Elk Run township; killed in action at Chickamauga, September 19, 1863.

Corporal Robert Ewing, New Lisbon; died of wounds received at Munforeboro, Tenn.

Corporal Jos. H. Wright, Fairfield township.

Musician Jerimiah E. Williams, Fairfield township.

Musician Peter W. Smith, Middleton township; promoted to sergeant.

Henry H. Arner, Fairfield township; discharged to enlist in Fourth U. S. battalion.

Henry H. Beck, Fairfield township.

Fisher A. Billingsley, Middleton township; discharged for disability, May 17, 1862.

Isaac Burlingame, Middleton township.

Robt. Boles, Fairfield township; died at Corinth, Miss., July 2, 1862.

Benj. F. Burcaw, Fairfield township; discharged for disability Jan. 18, 1862.

Lewis Bernstine, Fairfield township.

Chas. Castle, Fairfield township.

Jeremiah Cole, Centre township; discharged for disabality October 2, 1863.

James F. H. Cook, Fairfield township; Vet. Vo.; transferred to Department of the Cumberland by order.

Thomas C. Campbell, Unity township; died at Cheat Mountain, Va., November 16, 1861.

Jno. C. Dildine, Unity township.

Geo. L. Dix, Unity township, promoted to sergeant; discharged to enlist in Fourth U. S. Battalion.

Samuel F. Donaldson, Mahoning county, Vet. Vol.; transferred to Department of the Cumberland.

Fred Everhart, Mahoning county; discharged to enlist in Fourth U. S. Battalion.

Wm. English, Mahoning county; transferred to Department of the Cumberland.

Jas. S. Edsell, Mahoning county, Vet. Vol.; transferred to Department of the Cumberland.

Hiram Fasnacht, Mahoning county; discharged for disability, Aug. 8, 1861.

Chambers O. Gamble, Mahoning county, Vet. Vol.; transferred to Department of the Cumberland.

John Grose, Mahoning county; transferred to Inv. Corps August 5, 1863.

Cabel Garrett, Fairfield township; discharged by order.

Geo. W. Hannon, Fairfield township.

Isaac Jones, Mahoning county; died at Nashville, Tenn., March 26, 1862.

John Little, Mahoning county; promoted to sergeant.

Rufus L. Ney, Fairfield township, Vet. Vo.; transferred.

Benj. F. Peterson, Fairfield township; discharged for disability Jan. 18, 1862.

Irwin G. Porter, Fairfield township; promoted to corporal.

Wm. Roller, Mahoning county.

John H. Roberts, Fairfield township; promoted to corporal.

Samuel Richey, Fairfield township; discharged by order.

Peter J. Shuster, Mahoning county; died at Cheat Mountain, Va., October 9, 1861.

Benj. F. Taylor, Middleton township; discharged to enlist in Fourth U. S. Artillery.

Sylvanus F. Tullis, Elk Run township.

Richard B. Tullis, Elk Run township; transferred to Inv. Corps Jan. 13, 1864.

Jno. E. Taylor, Middleton township; died January 7, 1863, of wounds received at Stone River.

Jno. I. Vanderslice, Fairfield township; discharged for disability August 19, 1862.

Jos. M. Woldorf, Fairfield township; transferred to Inv. Corps Sept. 1, 1863.

Jno. Weyle, Springfield township, Mahoning county; died at Nashville, Tenn., April 1, 1862.

Jno. Wheland, Mahoning county; promoted to corporal.
Geo. Walters, Fairfield township.

Twenty-Seventh Regiment, O. V. I.

First Lieutenant William M. Vogleson, Columbiana; promoted to captain and A. A. G. July 24, 1861.

Thirty-Fifth Regiment, O. V. I.

Christian Ballheimer, Fairfield township.

Forty-First Regiment, O. V. I.—Company F.

First Lieutenant Ephraim S. Holloway, Columbiana, Fairfield township; enlisted October 10, 1861; promoted to captain September 8, 1862; major November 26, 1864; lieutenant colonel March 18, 1865; colonel May 31, 1865; brevet brigadier general March 13, 1865; mustered out with regiment November 27, 1865.

Corporal Alex Bushong, Fairfield township; discharged for disability November 4, 1862.

Alex Lehman, Fairfield township; died April 7, 1862, of wounds received at Shiloh.

Joe Parrish, Fairfield township; killed in the battle of Stone River, December 31, 1862.

Sixty-First Regiment, O. V. I.—Company D

(From Columbiana, Fairfield Township, Ohio)

Sergeant James H. Bell, promoted to second lieutenant September 14, 1862; first lieutenant April 29, 1864; honorable discharge December 15, 1864.

Corporal Wm. Fesler; transferred to and mustered out of Eighty-second Volunteer Infantry with regiment; re-enlisted as veteran.

John Boyd.

Peter Good; discharged by order October 18, 1862.

Robt. D. Gray.

George Kipp.

Samuel Liddle, sick in hospital, Feb. 29, 1864.

Lemmel Little.

Edward Obenauf, died in hospital at Camp Dennison, O., January 11, 1864.

Lewis Obenauf, died in hospital at Camp Chase, O., June 2, 1862.

Chas. Onderkirk.

John Rank, killed in action at Freeman's Ford, Va., August 22, 1862.

Ephriam Sheelenberger; promoted to first sergeant and second lieutenant; mustered out with Eighty-second regiment as sergeant; re-enlisted as veteran.

Jacob A. Signer.

John Shafer, discharged by order (on date).

Jacob B. Stauffer.

(Consolidated with the Eighty-second Ohio Vet. Vol. Inf. at Goldsboro, N. C., March 31, 1865.

Seventy-Seventh Regiment, O. V. I.—Company E.

John Flickinger, Columbiana, Fairfield.

One Hundred and Fourth Regiment, O. V. I.—Company C.

Wm. W. Mitchell; mustered out at Greensboro, N. C., June 17, 1865.
Adam Yagala, Unity; in hospital in Knoxville, Tenn.; not mustered out.
Thos. Piper, Unity.

One Hundred and Fifteenth O. V. I.—Company H.

(From Columbiana, Fairfield Township)

Captain Abdiel Sturgeon; enlisted August 22, 1862; mustered out with regiment.

First Lieutenant Simeon Somers, Perry township; enlisted August 14, 1862; resigned March 1, 1864.

Second Lieutenant Henry H. Woods; enlisted August 11, 1864; mustered out with regiment.

Second Lieutenant Henry H. Glosser; enlisted September 9, 1862; promoted to lieutenant Co. E., August 24, 1864; mustered out with regiment.

Sergeant James A. Davidson; discharged for disability January 17, 1863.

Sergeant Henry H. Woods; promoted to second lieutenant August 11, 1864; mustered out with regiment.

Sergeant Geo. F. Arter, Salem township; promoted to U. S. Col. Inf.

Sergeant Fred Lease, Perry township; promoted to sergeant; mustered out June 22, 1865.

Sergeant Abner M. Fugate, Hanover township; promoted to first sergeant; mustered out June 22, 1865.

Corporal John M. Williams, Fairfield township; transferred to Co. B July 1, 1864.

Corporal Caleb M. Taylor, Salem , Perry township; promoted to sergeant; mustered out June 22, 1865.

Corporal Joe S. Stewart, Salem township; mustered out June 22, 1865.

Corporal David Havil, Fairfield township; mustered out June 22, 1865.

Corporal John B. McConnell, Fairfield township; mustered out June 22, 1865.

Corporal Henry E. Fuhrman, Beaver township; promoted to sergeant; mustered out June 22, 1865.

Corporal Samuel Groner, Salem township; mustered out June 22, 1865.

Corporal Alfred White, Perry township; mustered out June 22, 1865.

Edward W. Garrett, drummajor, Fairfield township; prisoner; killed by explosion on steamer "Sultana," Mississippi river, as exchange of prisoners was being made, April 27, 1865.

J. P. Andrews, Hanover township; mustered out June 22, 1865.

Jesse A. Ask, Fairfield township; mustered out June 22, 1865.

Geo. Beard, Fairfield township; promoted to corporal; mustered out June 22, 1865.

Wm. Brubaker, Fairfield township; mustered out June 22, 1865.

Jonas Bear, Beaver township, Mahoning county; mustered out June 22, 1865.

Chas. H. W. Beecher, musician, Beaver township; discharged to take first lieutenant in First U. S. Colored Heavy Artillery; died at Chattanooga, September 19, 1866.

Jesse P. Baker, Fairfield township; died of disease at Cincinnati, Ohio, April 17, 1863.

David Byers, New Lisbon, Centre township; mustered out June 22, 1865.

Samuel Buell, Salem township; mustered out June 22, 1865.

Daniel Bushong, Fairfield township; promoted to corporal; mustered out June 22, 1865.
Wm. H. Beyer, Salem township; mustered out June 22, 1865.
Sylvanus F. Buck, Fairfield township; mustered out June 22, 1865.
Lloyd D. Caldwalder, Salem; mustered out June 22, 1865.
Geo. W. Cole, Fairfield township; mustered out June 22, 1865.
Geo. Candle, Beaver township; mustered out June 22, 1865.
Noah Coblentz, Fairfield; discharged for wounds, December, 1862.
Samuel Clickner, New Lisbon; mustered out June 22, 1865.
David Dehoff, Fairfield township.
Joseph Dehoff, Fairfield township; mustered out June 22, 1865.
Samuel Dowder, Salem township; mustered out June 22, 1865.
Wm. Dean, Salem; finish of war; not mustered out with company.
Hugh W. Eaton, Fairfield township; mustered out June 22, 1865.
Thos. Eels, Middleton township; absent, sick; not mustered out with company.
Jesse Fesler, Fairfield township; trans. to Vet. Res. Corps, June 1, 1864.
Jacob Flickinger, Fairfield township; mustered out June 22, 1865.
David Freed, Fairfield township; mustered out June 22, 1865.
Emanuel Freed, Fairfield township; mustered out June 22, 1865.
Milton Freed, Fairfield township; died of disease at Maysville, Ky., October 25, 1863.
Edward Gibbons, Fairfield township.
David Grim, Fairfield township; discharged by order February 5, 1863.
Henry H. Getz, Fairfield; mustered out June 22, 1865.
Benedict Green, Salem township; mustered out June 22, 1865.
Wm. Green, Madison township; died of disease at Camp Chase, October 22, 1862.
John J. Harkness, Fairfield; mustered out June 22, 1865.
Oliver Holloway, Fairfield; mustered out June 22, 1865.
John Haeton, Fairfield; mustered out June 22, 1865.
Wm. Haecock, Butler township; mustered out June 22, 1865.
Wm. Halverstadt, Salem township; promoted to sergeant; mustered out June 22, 1865.
Michael W. Henry, Fairfield.
David W. Halverstadt, Salem township; mustered out June 22, 1865.
Samuel W. Halverstadt, Salem township; mustered out June 22, 1865.
Theo. I. Hoffman, Salem township; mustered out June 22, 1865.
Jos. Hisey, Fairfield township; mustered out June 22, 1865.
Geo. Kridler, Fairfield township; mustered out June 22, 1865.
John G. Kageriss, Fairfield township; mustered out June 22, 1865.
Mosheim Kendig; died of disease at Cincinnati, Ohio, August 24, 1863.
Lewis Kalnberg, Knox township; mustered out June 22, 1865.
John Kirchter, Unity township; mustered out June 22, 1865.
Oliver Limebach, Salem; mustered out June 22, 1865.
Josia Lehman, Fairfield; mustered out June 22, 1865.
Alex Lowery, Salem; lost a leg in battle; discharged.
Geo. Leaf, Fairfield; mustered out June 22, 1865.
Amos Miller, Fairfield; accidentally shot; died November 9, 1864.
Joel Oberholtzer, Fairfield; mustered out June 22, 1865.
Joseph T. Porter, Fairfield; mustered out June 22, 1865.

Geo. Roninger, Fairfield; mustered out June 22, 1865.
Hosea Rymer, Fairfield; promoted to corporal; mustered out June 22, 1865.
Benj. Richey, Fairfield; mustered out June 22, 1865.
Harman E. Ruggy, Fairfield; mustered out June 22, 1865.
Edward H. Pearl, discharged for disability, January 4, 1864.
James H. Scott, Fairfield; mustered out June 22, 1865.
Hezekiah Scott, Fairfield; mustered out June 22, 1865.
Chas. Snyder, Fairfield; mustered out June 22, 1865.
Enos Seachrist; mustered out June 22, 1865.
Franklin Schooley; mustered out June 22, 1865.
Daniel L. Sharpnack, Salem township; mustered out June 22, 1865.
Samuel S. Switzer; mustered out June 22, 1865.
Thos. I. Shively, Butler township; mustered out June 22, 1865.
Christian Shabe, Perry township; mustered out June 22, 1865.
Edward Steel, Perry township; mustered out June 22, 1865.
Elias Steel; mustered out June 22, 1865.
Geo. D. Smith, Salem township; mustered out June 22, 1865.
Jonathan Trucksis; mustered out June 22, 1865.
Chas. Tatum, Perry township; mustered out June 22, 1865.
Isaac Thomas, Butler township; mustered out June 22, 1865.
Robert V. Votaw, Salem township; promoted to corporal; mustered out June 22, 1865.
Garret Williamson, Fairfield; mustered out June 22, 1865.
Henry Williamson, Fairfield; mustered out June 22, 1865.
Mahlon Williamson, Fairfield; mustered out June 22, 1865.
Lewis Wunderlin, Farfield; mustered out June 22, 1865.
Jeremiah Wildasin, Fairfield; mustered out June 22, 1865.
Abram B. Wright, Fairfield; mustered out June 22, 1865.
Milton Whitmer, Fairfield; mustered out June 22, 1865.
John S. Weaver, Salem township; mustered out June 22, 1865.
Francis M. Webb, Salem, Perry township; mustered out June 22, 1865.

One Hundred and Forty-Third Regiment, O. V. I., "National Guards"

Company F

(From Fairfield Township)

Captain Benjamin S. Wright.
First Lieutenant Leonard D. Holloway.
Second Lieutenant John W. Detwiler.
First Sergeant Albert Shields.
Sergeants Eli Sturgeon, John F. Woods, Edmund Ferral, Joseph Wallace.
Corporals John J. Bushong, Daniel Strickler, Geo. Heaton, Albert W. Voglesong, David S. Grim, Jeremiah Groner, Levi H. Esterly, Israel H. Meredick.
Musicians Edwin McCregor, Daniel M. Smith.
Wagoner Alfred Heacock.
Melancthon H. Augustine, Wm. Augustine.
Jas. Arb; transferred to Co. I.
Oakley H. Bailey.

Thomas H. Biery, absent on sick leave; not mustered out with company.

Franklin H. Barnhart, Alpheus A. Bushong, Alex Bushong, Jacob Baer; discharged for disability.

John T. Barclay, Conrad Brenner, Rufus Cope, David Crawford, John D. Compton, Silas S. Crow, Jacob Deemer, Nathaniel M. Engle, Hinchman Engle, Jos. Ferguson.

Simpson Ferney; discharged for disability.

Samuel B. Holloway, Wm. D. Hendricks, Daniel Hisey, Thomas F. Holloway, Nicholas B. Howlett, Franklin B. Keyser, Geo. Kapp, Geo. Lower, absent on sick leave; not mustered out with company.

Henry S. Miller, Conrad J. Mark, Winfield Marlatt, James K. Moore, Matthew McMichael.

Jas. McGee, Liverpool township; transferred to Co. I.

Nathaniel Martin, Liverpool township; transferred to Co. I.

Frederick Nagle, Liverpool township; transferred to Co. I.

John Shaffer, Henry Swigert, David Seachrist; discharged for disability.

Geo. Shifley, John Stumpf, John Stiver; discharged for disability.

Albert Shenkle, Liverpool township; transferred to Co. I.

W. B. Scott, Liverpool township; transferred to Co. I.

John Sherwood, Liverpool township; transferred to Company I.

John H. Trotter.

Andrew Thomas; discharged for disability.

John Witt, absent without leave since May 15, 1864.

Wilson Walker, Liverpool township; transferred to Co. B.

Frederick Zerbrugg.

One Hundred and Seventy-Sixth Regiment, O. V. I.

Company D was organized at Alilance, O., and mustered in at Camp Chase September 12, 1864, to serve one year. It was mustered out of service June 14, 1865, by order of the War Department.

First Lieutenant Geo. W. Beck, Fairfield township; resident Feb. 16, 1865.

Corporal James Howell; mustered out with company.

Second Maryland Regiment—Company D

Private Wm. Boyd, a citizen of Columbiana, O.

One Hundred and Twentieth Regiment, O. V. I.

G. S. Metzger, Columbiana, O., volunteer physician.

Mr. J. E. Vogleson, Columbiana, O., volunteer nurse.

Sixth Pennsylvania Heavy Artillery—Company C

Jacob Schaber, Allegheny, Pa., became a citizen of Columbiana, Ohio.

In 1851 W. Anthony Smith built a two-story brick flouring mill on his property on the northwest corner of Elm street and the newly layed Pittsburg, Fort Wayne and Chicago railroad. This mill was supplied with three runs of stone, operated by an eighty horse-power engine, and was long known as the "City Mills."

Some years later the "City Mills" was owned and operated by Pierce and Cramer, then by Weaver and Peoples, and by Augustus Miller, and in 1875 Conrad Theiss bought the mill. It was then continued under the firm name of "The Eureka Flour Mills." On May 6, 1884, this mill was burned down. The four sons, Philip, Peter, Henry, and Fred, were then taken in as partners and a three-story brick grist mill was erected, March 9, 1885. Soon after Mr. Christ Kuegle became identified as a partner, and the Eureka Flour Mills was run under the firm name of Theiss, Kuegle & Co., until July, 1898, when Mr. Kuegle retired from the firm. The four brothers then continued the business under the firm name of Theis Bros. Mills. In

Anthony Smith

1903 Philip withdrew, leaving his three brothers to continue the work. In November, 1904, Peter withdrew. This left Henry and Fred to continue the mill work. In July, 1910, Henry purchased Fred's half interest in the mill. Henry Theiss as sole proprietor continued the business until May 23, 1911,

when the Theiss Flour Mills was totally destroyed by fire. The loss aggregated $40,000. The Brungard Brothers soon after purchased the site and built the present three-story, buff-colored brick building, the same size as the Theiss Flour Mills. This mill is supplied with the latest and best improved machinery andit is the most up-to-date, 100-barrel capacity mill in the country.

The Press

The first paper was published in Columbiana in 1857 by Revs. Kurtz and Winter. This publication, "Gospel Visitor," was a German and English monthly devoted to the interests of their society—the Dunkards. In 1866 the office was removed to Dayton, from its rooms on the northeast corner of Main street and the public square.

In the spring of 1858 Black and Watson begun the publication of The Telegraph. This was the first local newspaper published in Columbiana. It lasted only twenty-four weeks and died about the month of September.

In September, 1858, C. H. M. Beecher began the publication of the "Columbiana Ledger." For some time R. L. King was editor. Later Isaac (Dad) Hill filled the position, while Mr. Beecher was in the army. Upon his return he had the presses removed to Pittsburg.

In the summer of 1861 R. L. King began the publication of the "Columbiana Chronicle." It continued for six months and was suspended.

Columbiana had now been without a secular paper for ten years. April 1, 1870, several enterprising citizens employed J. M. Hutton as editor and on Thursday, April 14, published the first number of the "Independent Register." Five numbers were issued when the property passed into the hands of the Washington Printing company, composed of Gen. E. S. Holloway, J. B. Powell, A. Sturgeon, J. Esterly, and W. R. Knowles. Geo. Duncan was employed as editor. Mr. Duncan was a lawyer, but besides his practice, he proved himself a very efficient editor, remaining in the village until February, 1871. For seven months R. G. Mosgrove pushed the editorial quill. The company then sold the office and fixtures to Frank M. Atterholt and Noah Nold, but after a few issues Atterholt sold his interests to Gen. E. S. Holloway. Holloway and Nold continued the publication until May, 1872, when Gen. E. S. Holloway became editor and sole proprietor. In April, 1877, his sons, John W. and Orlando T., became associated with him and continued the business under the firm name of Holloway & Sons. September, 1879, John Flaugher became proprietor. He continued the publication until his death in 1896. Harry Garret then purchased the plant and continued the publication until 1897, when it was sold to Elmer Firestone, who continued the publication a few months, when the "Independent Register" was suspended.

July 14, 1875, L. and T. S. Arnold established the "Columbiana True Press," and published this paper until August, 1887, when Thomas S. Arnold, who had been sole proprietor for some time, moved the office to Leetonia, Ohio. John G. Beatty was associate editor for several years.

In 1890 the "Columbiana Ledger" was established by a stock company, with George McLaughlin as managing editor. In 1894 the publication was continued by Arthur Edgerton. In 1895 Newell and Shingler became proprietors and the publication was continued under the firm name until Shingler's death in 1904, when Mr. H. O. Newell became editor and sole proprietor.

The "New Moon," a monthly press periodical, published by Ira D. Slotter, a job printer, had its birth in February, 1890, and lasted about three years. The home of this little paper was in a room in the Slotter block on the northwest corner of Main and Friend streets. In December, 1894, C. E. Wolfgang bought the job office and did job printing for the public until April, 1896, when he sold out to Wilson Edgerton.

Thursday, September 1, 1898, Wilson Edgerton began the publication of

"The Independent." In 1901 C. P. Moreland became associated with Edgerton. The publication was enlarged. For want of more room the office was moved from the room in the Agnew block to the more commodious rooms over S. S. Weaver's Feed store, on Main street. In 1903 Edgerton and Moreland sold out to G. E. Koch, who continued its publication about six weeks, when he sold out to Newell and Shingler, thus absolving "The Independent" into their publication, "The Columbiana Ledger." Mr. Koch continuing in his former occupation as job printer, located again in his own office building next door to his home on Elm street.

Other papers heralding current events in this locality were published at different times by Adam Weaver and George G. Chamberlain.

The Bar

The following members of the Bar of Columbiana county have resided in the city of Columbiana, Ohio:

Wm. Orr practiced in Columbiana for a few months during the year 1860. He moved to Salineville.

John D. King came to Columbiana from Warren, Ohio, in 1862. He practiced in Columbiana and Mahoning counties for five years. In June, 1867, he moved to Kenton, Ohio.

George S. Duncan came to Columbiana in 1865, was admitted to the bar in 1866, and commenced practice early in 1867. He moved to Monroeville, Ohio, in 1874.

Chas. D. Dickinson was admitted to the bar August 28, 1872, in Lisbon, Ohio, at a session of the District Court, and commenced practice March 20, 1873, in Columbiana.

Frederick A. Witt, a native of Fairfield township, was admitted to the bar August 31, 1874, at Akron, Ohio, and practiced in Columbiana from April 1, 1875, to 1909.

John G. Beatty was born in Charlestown, Mass., September 9, 1826. He emigrated to Pennsylvania in 1833, and to Ohio in 1873. He was admitted to the bar September 1, 1874, at Akron, Ohio, and commenced practice in Columbiana a few days later. He died in July, 1902.

Ephriam S. Holloway was born in Fairfield township, July 27, 1833, and was admitted to the bar April 11, 1877, at Columbus, Ohio, and commenced practice in Columbiana November 1, 1877. He died September 15, 1895.

Ezra B. Nye graduated from the Cincinnati Law School in the spring of 1894. Was admitted to the bar of Ohio the same spring. Commenced practice in Columbiana in 1898, in the office of his brother, H. G. Bye, vacated. He remained here about two years and a half.

Fred D. Lodge was born near State Center, Marshall county, Iowa, December 19, 1875. He was brought to a farm near Columbiana when but six months old. He graduated from the law school at Ada, Ohio, was admitted to the bar in June, 1900, and commenced practice in Columbiana a few days later. He remained until 1906. During this time he was solicitor of the village. Now engaged in the dry goods business, having succeeded The H. H. Smith's Sons Co. in that line.

John B. Morgan was born near Leetonia, Ohio, April 6, 1869; admitted to the bar at Columbus, Ohio, October 5, 1892, and since that date he has practiced law at Leetonia, Ohio. About the first of February, 1906, he established a branch office at Columbiana, and continued same for about two years.

W. O. Wallace was born in Unity township, Columbiana county, May 12, 1881. Graduated from East Palestine High School in June, 1898. Graduated in scientific course in June, 1900; in classical course in 1901. Graduated in Law, Missouri State University, 1903. Admitted in Missouri in 1903. Postgraduate course graduate in 1904. Admitted to bar in Ohio in 1904. Commenced practice of law in Columbiana, Ohio, on November 1, 1906.

H. W. Hammond born in Madison township, Columbiana, Ohio; received his schooling in a rural school of Madison township named Pleasant Valley (known to the boys who went to school with him as "Buzzards Glory"). His higher education was received in the schools of Lisbon, Ohio, and in Valparaiso University and in the Ohio Northern University. He was graduated from the latter university in the year 1910, was admitted to the bar of Ohio on June 24 of that year. He opened a law office in Columbiana during the fore part of October, 1910, and has continued actively in the practice of law since that date.

Bands and Musical Organizations in Columbiana

First Brass Band of 1840.

Leader, Jacoba. Members: Ruben Strickler, John Young, Ab Sturgeon, Jacob Flickinger, Frederick Stiver, Ab. Fitzpatrick, Levi Esterly, Chas. Young, Asa Garwood, John Koch, Ab. Vogleson.

Orchestra of 1856

Leader, Wm. Lamb. Members: David Keister, Eli Sturgeon, Isaac Havil, John Barrows, John Hollar.

String Band of 1858.

Leader, Wm. Lamb. Members: Joe Seachrist, Aaron Overholt, John Snyder, David Keister.

Orchestra of 1870

Leader, Wm. Lamb. Members: Chas. Dickinson, David Keister, John Webb; pianist, Emma Lamb.

Second Brass Band of 1875-78

Leader, Miller. Members: John Webb, Josiah Rohrbaugh, Isaac Havil, John Early, John Sturgeon, A. C. Bell, Albert Sturgeon, J. C. Groner, Chas. Beecher, David Keister.

Orchestra of 1876-77.

Leader, Wm. Lamb. Members: John Rohrbaugh, Paul Koch, John Webb, Josiah Rohrbaugh, David Keister, George G. Webb.

Webb's Orchestra of 1877.

Leader, J. M. Webb. Members: Jos. Wining, David Keister, Paul Koch, Andy Wiggins.

Orchestra of 1878

Leader, Geo. Knox. Members: David Keister, Nathan Gleckler, Henry Koch.

Third Brass Band of 1879

Leader, Jacob Rohrer.

This year the members of second brass band accept the names of a number of new members, viz.: George Webb, Wm. Mitchela, Fred Blecker, Andy Lindsay, David Havil, James O'Rourke, Ab. Morlan.

The leader of the band afterwards became the band master of the Pittsburgh Great Western Band.

J. C. Groner constructed a band wagon and the band would play as far away as New Castle, Pa.

Fourth Brass Band of 1880

Leaders, Paul Koch and Wm. Mitchela. Members: Clark McClun, Wm. Slutter, Chas. Slutter, Frank Mitchela, Elmer Augustine, Si Wonsitler, Thomas Johnson, Harry Slutter, John Rohrbaugh, Selby Webb, Jas. Fetzer. Ed. I. Snyder, Wm. Fesler, David Keister, Wm. Hum.

Orchestra of 1882

Leader, Wm. Mitchela. Members: Wm. Mitchel, Alba Slutter, Samuel Buffinger, David Keister, Sy. Wonsettler.

Webb's Orchestra of 1888.

Leader, J. M. Webb. Members: David Keister, Selby Webb, Claude Wilkinson; pianist, Mrs. Dora Webb.

Drum Corps of 1896-1900

Leader, P. H. Holloway. Members: Fifers, L. Myers, Hosea Shaffer, Thomas Cope, C. C. Wilkinson, Fred Staley, C. E. Wolfgang.

Tenor Drums—Hal Wilkinson, Wm. Miller, Frank Williamson, Clarence Snyder, John Evans, Walter Beck, Frank Fesler, Chas. Sample, Bert Sample, Carl Yagley.

Bass Drums—Ralph Myers, W. G. Kenney, Ed. Hinkle.

Sixth Brass Band of 1897

Leader, Frederick Thoman. Drummajor, G. B. Kyser. Members: Harvey Vanskiver, David Whitehouse, Chas. and Albert Troll, John Wingard, Fred Lindsay, Terzah Renkenberger, Raymonod Mathers, Howard Martin, Al. McBride, Chas. Keller, Frank Kyser, Elmer Lower, Ralph Keller, Clarence Wining, Harvey Keller, Thomas Cope, Adin Mather, Arthur Lewis, Earl McCurry, John Longbottom, Wm. Haag, Roy Holloway, Harold Breckenridge.

Fifth Brass Band of 1900

Leader, John Webb. Members: John Weikert, Ira Stahl, Selby Webb, John Longbottom, Jacob Longbottom, Norman Floor, George Overholt, Fitch Sitler, John Esterly, Al. Cover, Arthur Lenning, Benj. Mathers, Hosea Shaffer.

Lyric Orchestra of 1907

Leader, Harrold Breckenridge. Members: Wilbur H. Rogers, Albert Heston, John Biddison. Pianist, Miss Lucile Breckenridge.

Arcadia Orchestra of 1911-12

Leader, W. H. Rogers. Members: Al. Heston, Harrold Breckenridge, John Biddison, Homer Troll. Pianist, Leo Holloway.

Churches and Religious Societies

About 1813 a Reformed missionary from the east, whose name was Mahnesmith, visited Columbiana and held catechetical instructions in a small log tavern on the west side of the public square. It is said "some one, after hearing one of his forceful sermons, lightly remarked to another as they were passing out, 'Today it thundered again.' "

Mahnesmith, who was at the door shaking hands, giving a parting word of cheer to the retiring congregation, instantly replied: "If it only would strike in too." He continued his labors at Columbiana, with work in Mahoning county, until about 1830.

Friends Orthodox Branch

Among the first settlers of Fairfield township, the Friends largely predominated. In the summer of 1803 a delegation was appointed by the Red Stone Quarterly Meeting of Pennsylvania to visit the new settlement and organize what is now known as "The Middleton Monthly Meeting of the Society of Orthodox Friends." It is recorded that one of the delegates, who came on this mission, was Jonas Cattel, who was then seventy years old. About 1818 a small log meeting house was built on the lot now owned by Royal Conkey on Elm street, for the accommodation of members of their faith who resided in the northern part of the township. The east portion of the meeting grounds was reserved to bury their dead.

This house contained at first but one room. We are told that on one occasion, when a business meeting was held, that bed quilts were hung so as to partition off another room. In 1832 the members of the Orthodox branch became Hicksites and the meetings were then held by that society.

Hicksite Branch.

The Hicksite Friends of Columbiana was organized in 1832 when the membership of the Orthodox Branch decided to become known as Hicksites. The members were Lot Holms, Samuel Nichols, Thomas Mercer, Morton Dixon, Stacy Nichols, Cyrus Mercer, William Nichols, John Armstrong, Thomas Wickersham, Moses Emery, and their wives. The Orthodox Meeting House on the east side of Elm street was now moved to the northwest corner of Elm and Friend streets, and known thereafter as the Hicksite Meeting House.

Wm. Nichols

Wm. Nichols and wife, Kysander, were recommended ministers, and John Armstrong and Thomas Wickersham were occasional preachers.

The regular monthly meetings were discontinued in 1867. Since that time the members became so few that the society was practically extinct, though still retaining its right to the church property, until February 8, 1868, when the premises passed from the Middleton Meeting of Friends to the Salem Monthly Meeting of Friends. For many years the old church remained unused. June 9, 1883, the town lot upon which the old church stands was sold to Adam Kaidaiseh, and on February 14, 1906, the piece of real estate fronting on the east side of Elm street and south of Friend street, which was known as the Friends Burial Grounds, was disposed of by the Salem Monthly Meeting of Friends to Royal Conkey.

The School and Meeting House Society

In the year 1815 a house of hewed logs was built on the now northeast corner of Main and Pittsburgh streets. This was built for church and school. Mr. Mahnesmith now had a permanent house to preach in. The ground was donated to the School and Meeting House Society by Joshua Dixon. The conditions of fellowship required in this society were: "A practical conformity to the principles of impartial equity, and that every member shall be considered as possessing in himself an original and inalienable right to believe and worship God as his own conscience may dictate without being called into question by any other member." It was "allowed for any licensed preacher that preaches the gospel of Jesus Christ in purity, to preach in the above said meeting house, if he makes application to the trustees, and should it happen that application should be made for two preachers in one day, let one preach in the forenoon and the other in the afternoon, so that none may meet with disappointment."

The following names of associate subscribers, with the amount subscribed by each, and in what received, are appended to the articles of association.

Names of Associate Subscribers	Money	Produce		Work	In What Received Materials
Michael Croxen	$10.	$5.11	¼	6 days	
Abraham Fox	6.	2.35	½	6 days	
Christopher	x 10.	2.25		6 days	
John Bushong	6.	6.00		6 days	
Frederick Keller	6.	5.62	½	6 days	
Peter Bushong	8.	0.83	¼	6 days	
Michael Esterly	6.	2.37	½	6 days	

Joseph Keekly	6.	6.00			
William Bushong	15.	....		in boards, ash, and poplar	
George Grimm	3.	3.00			
William Case	5.	5.00			
Gottlieb x	3. .	1.00			
Samuel Dewees	1.	....			
Geenyoe Mikkens	2.	2.00			
Frederick Harman	1.	1.00			
John Windle	3.	3.00			
Hugh Chain	1.	1.00			
John L. Desselems		....	3 days	not paid	
Daniel Hardman	3.	....	......	in boards, poplar	
Joseph Geisinger	1.50	1.50			
John Frederick	1.50	1.50			

x Signed in German.

The Lutheran and Reformed Church

It seemed that for a few years the Lutheran and Reformed congregations worshiped together harmoniously, and in 1822, though separately organized, with their own pastor, elders, and deacons, they erected a union church. In order to facilitate the building, a joint meeting of the congregations annually elected the trustees, a secretary, and a treasurer. The house was built of brick, with galleries, and occupied the present site of the Grace church. Rev. Hewet became the pastor for the Lutheran congregation, and Rev. Sonnedecker for the Reformed congregation.

Reformed Ministers	Lutheran Ministers
1822-45—Rev. Sonnedecker.	1824-38—Rev. Hewet.
1845-53—Rev. Palsgrove.	1838-42—Rev. Hoelsche.
1853-58—Rev. Aaron Warner.	1842-45—Rev. Siegele.
1858-59—Rev. Roemer.	1845-57—Rev. Mueller.
1860-70—Rev. James Rinehart.	1857-61—Rev. Schladermund.
	1861-69—Rev. F. Nouffer.

The Methodist Episcopal Church of Columbiana, Ohio

The Methodist Episcopal Church of this place was built in 1834 on the corner of Main Cross and Elm streets, under the trusteeship of John Vogleson and John Fitzpatrick, as a free church to all Christian denominations when not occupied by them, and was dedicated by Rev. Father Swasey, one of the pioneers of Methodism of this country. It was then a four-weeks circuit, embracing Salem, New Lisbon, East Liverpool, Crawfords Mills, Harts, Burts and with almost daily appointments within the bounds of the circuit, with a salary of $200.00 a year for a man with a family, or $100.00 a year for a single man. This house of worship was used until 1859, when the present brick edific on Main street was built. The present M. E. church was commenced in 1859, finished and dedicated Sabbath, August 5, 1860, by Davis W. Clark, who was later chosen a bishop. The building committee was composed of Wm. Wright, Daniel Deemer, Daniel Stouffer, Isaac Groff, Enoch C. Cloud, George Freed, and Samuel Sheets, who drew up the following proposal:

The Trustees of the M. E. Church in Columbiana proposed to the citizens of this place, that if they will subscribe liberally to the erection of a more commodious house of worship in the town of Columbiana for the use of the M. E. Church and those who worship with them,

That we will deed the old church to the town council of Columbiana for a Town Hall.

We, the undersigned, agree to pay the sum annexed to our several names to build a House of Worship in the town of Columbiana, County of Columbiana, Ohio, for the use of the members of the M. E. Church and those who desire to worship with them.

Payments to be made to the trustees of said church or their authorized agents in three equal payments.

Viz.: one-third on or before the 20th day of May, 1859; one-third on or before the 20th day of September, 1859; and balance one third on or before the 20th day of January, 1860.

Subscribed Names

Daniel Stouffer	$100.00	Jeremiah Groner	25.00
Daniel Deemer	100.00	Jacob Beard	25.00
Richard Davis	100.00	David Greenamyer	25.00
John Fitzpatrick	100.00	Jonathan Fesler, Sr.	25.00
Wm. M. Wright	100.00	George Lamb	25.00
Isaac Groff	100.00	R. H. Carpenter	25.00
George Freed	50.00	Jacob B. Esterly	25.00
Samuel Sheets	50.00	Abtil Sturgeon	25.00
Wm. Wallace	50.00	H. M. Lorrence	25.00
Jonathan Esterly	50.00	Wm. Sturgeon	25.00
Thos. Thurston	50.00	Geo. Mankin	25.00
Joseph Wallace	50.00	J. J. Schauwecker	25.00
John Baerd	25.00	Jacob Gilbert	25.00
Eliabeth Sturgeon	25.00	Wm. M. Vogleson	25.00
Joseph Hively	25.00	Wm. A. Bushong	25.88
John Deemer	20.00	David DeHoff	10.00
John Winch	25.00	Jesse M. Allen	10.00
Elizabeth Kemble	25.00	Geo. Herring	10.00
Lafayett Stuckman	25.00	Hiram Heck	5.00
David Havil	25.00	Jacob Heck	5.00
M. Wesley Henry	15.00	Margaret Bradfield	5.00
George Roninger	15.00	John Compton	5.00
Wm. Fesler	15.00	John Cronk	5.00
Sarah Hiner	15.00	Wm. Cluck	5.00
E. C. Cloud	12.00	Wm. Steel	5.00
Josiah Lehman	15.00	Chas. Snyder	5.00
Albasena Cloud	12.00	Aaron Overholdt	5.00
David Deroads	15.00	Eunice Bishop	5.00
Wm. Stevenson	10.00	Mrs. Sarah Wolfe	5.00
David Strickler	10.34	Mrs. Sophia Kleckler	5.00
John Esterly, Jr.	14.00	Miss Mary Devitt	5.00
John Esterly, Sr.	15.00	John Michelly	5.00
Chas. Flodding	10.00	Wm. W. Orr	5.00
Jacob Seachrist	10.00	George Smith	5.00
Edward Flickinger	10.00	Harry Flickinger	5.00
Moses Coblentz	10.00	A. W. Vogleson	5.00
Beecher and Hill	10.00	Simeon Hardman (in goods)	5.00
Geo. Miller, farmer	10.00	Mrs. Sarah Boyer	5.00

David Witter	5.00	Adam Lentz	5.00
David Neidig	2.16	Elias Royer	1.00
Geo. Hartner	1.00	Henry Seachrist	4.27
Wesley Kemble	3.50		

The deed, the church trustees then gave to the village council, reads as follows:

Deed to the Building Given to the Town

Know all men by these presents, that we, Daniel Deemer, Daniel Stouffer, William M. Wright, Isaac Grooff, Enoch C. Cloud, Samuel Sheets, and George Freed, trustees in trust of the Methodist Episcopal Church at Columbiana, Columbiana County, Ohio, in consideration of one dollar in hand paid by Jonathan Esterly, David Scott, Jacob Beard and their associates in council, and as trustees in trust of the Incorporated Village of Columbiana, Ohio, and to their successors in office, forever, have bargained and sold and do hereby grant, bargain and sell and convey unto the said Jonathan Esterly, David Scott, Jacob Beard, and their associates in council as trustees in trust of the Incorporated Village of Columbiana, Ohio, and their successors in office, forever, the following described premises situated in the Village of Columbiana, Columbiana County, Ohio, and described as follows:

Being the north part of lot number fifty-nine (59) in the original plot of said village, fronting sixty (60) feet on the Petersburg street (East Cross street) and as far south as to include the building, being sixty feet square, more or less, with all the appurtenances thereunto belonging, reserving, however, the right of way for ingress and agress to and from the burying ground in rear of building. The above conveyed premises shall be under control of the town council, who shall act as trustees in trust and have charge and control of the premises for the general benefit of the citizens of the Village of Columbiana and vicinity, said building shall be forever free under the management and control of the Trustees as a Town Hall and Public Preaching for all Christian denominations.

In testimony whereof the said Daniel Deemer, Daniel Stouffer, William M. Wright, Isaac Groff, Enoch C. Cloud, Samuel Sheets and George Freed, have hereunto set their hands and seals this twenty-eighth day of August in the year of our Lord, one thousand eight hundred and sixty.

(Here are the signatures of the trustees).

                       Daniel Stouffer,   seal
                       Daniel Deemer,   seal
                       Enoch C. Cloud,   seal
                       Wm. M. Wright,   seal
                       George Freed,   seal
                       Samuel Sheets,   seal
                       Isaac Groff,   seal.

Signed, sealed, and acknowledged in the presence of Wm. Lamb, George Lamb. The State of Ohio, Columbiana County, ss.

Before me, George Lamb, a Justice of the Peace, in and for said county, personally appeared the above named Daniel Stouffer, Daniel Deemer, Enoch C. Cloud, William M. Wright, George Freed, Samuel Sheets, and Isaac Groff, and acknowledged the signing and sealing of the above conveyance to be their voluntary act and deed this 28th day of August, A. D. 1860.

                            George Lamb, J. P.

The pastors of the church since having been detached from the appointments in the southern part of the county have been as follows:

1854-55—Rev. J. Ansley.
1855 —Rev. J. Ansley and Rev. Pollock.
1856 —Rev. Geo. Cook and J. D. Turner.
1857-58—Rev. G. D. Kinnear.
1859 —Rev. D. Hess and Rev. L. S. Keagle.
1860 —Rev. D. Hess and Rev. M. S. Kendig.
1861 —Rev. J. McCarty and Rev. M. Long.
1863 —Rev. G. D. Kinnear and Rev. L. Payne.
1864 —Rev. J. Burbidge and Rev. E. M. Wood.
1865 —Rev. A. J. Rich and Rev. J. H. Coulee.
1866-67—Rev. R. Cunningham and Rev. D. Morneyer, and Rev. J. McConnell.
1871 —Rev. T. S. Hodgson.
1872-73—Rev. Wm. Darby.
1874 —Rev. J. J. Hays.
1875 —Rev. J. J. Moore.
1876-77—Rev. A. E. Ward.
1878 —Rev. C. H. Edwards.
1878-80—Rev. C. H. Edwards.
1881-82—Rev. H. Appleton.
1883-85—Rev. P. H. Edmonds.
1886 —Rev. S. W. McClure.
1887 —Rev. T. J. Ream.
1888 —Rev. I. D. McHenry.
1889-91—Rev. H. A. Cobbledick.
1892-93—Rev. S. Y. Kennedy.
1894 —Rev. J. T. Morton.
1895 —Rev. J. T. Morton and G. L. Davis.
1896 98—Rev. G. L. Davis.
1899-00— Rev. J. W. Satterthwaite.
1901 —Rev. Thos. Elliot.
1902 —Rev. Thos. Elliot and A. A. Brown.
1903 —Rev. A. A. Brown.
1904-05—Rev. J. M. Carr.
1906-08—Rev. Jason B. Manley.
1909 —Rev. John W. Moore.

The present church membership numbers 300. Mr. R. S. Breckenridge is superintendent of the Sabbath School, which has a membership of 300.

Methodist Episcopal Church

1885—A company of ladies of the Methodist Church met at the home of Mrs. James Dalzell, December 15, 1885. At the close of this meeting it was unanimously decided to hold similar gatherings. On Fberuary 24, 1886, the Ladies' Aid Society of the M. E. Church met at the home of Mrs. B. Stouffer and organized with 52 members. The officers were as follows: President, Mrs. P. H. Edmonds; vice-president, Mrs. Samuel Crouse; secretary, Miss M. A. Augustine; treasurer, Mrs. Isaiah Flickinger. Since the General Conference has given the Ladies' Aid of the M. E. Church of Columbiana a standing in the Quarterly Conference, every lady member of the church is considered a member of the present organization. The present officers are as follows: Prsident, Miss M. A. Augustine; vice-president, Mrs. H. M. Keister; secretary, Mrs. Isaiah Flickinger; treasurer, Mrs. Aaron Overholt.

1895—A class of children was taught in the M. E. Church as early as 1895, by Mrs. J. T. Morton, and later by Mrs. G. L. Davis. May 4, 1902, chapter No. 7986 of the Junior Epwoth League was organized. The present membership is 57. The superintendent is Miss Elizabeth Flickinger, and the assistant superintendent is Miss Mary A. Buzard.

1911—On the evening of February 22, 1911, a Brotherhood of the Methodist Church of Columbiana became a chapter of the "Methodist Brotherhood." On March 13, 1911 an election was held at the home of Rev. Dr. J. W. Moore. The first officers elected at this meeting were as follows: President, Theodore Theiss; vice-president, W. H. Rogers; secretary, Vincent C. Basinger; treasurer, W. H. Boyer; chaplain, L. E. Harman. The Brotherhood has had the pleasure of hearing many clean and interesting lectures by some very prominent and learned Methodist speakers.

The Grace Reformed Church

A disruption had arisen between the members of the Reformed and Lutheran churches and in 1867 the Reformed people bought out the interests of the Lutheran congregation in the church built in 1822 and the following year erected a fine brick edifice, with basement. This building they named "The Grace Reformed Church." In 1870 seventy persons were admitted to membership. Rev. Rinehart now closed his pastorate and Rev. Henry Hilbish took his place as the Grace Reformed pastor. The pastors to the church are as follows:

Grace Reformed Church

1870-72—Rev. Henry Hilbish.
1872-78—Rev. John M. Kendig.
1878 —Rev. H. Spangler.
1880-83—Rev. J. H. Bomberger, became ill in 1884 and was in Florida one year and a half. In 1886 he returned to take charge of his pastorate again.
1884-86—Rev. J. Learch.
1886-90—Rev. J. H. Bomberger.
1890-91—Rev. Parley E. Zartman.
1891 98—Rev. J. H. Bomberger.
1898-02—Rev. A. V. Casselman.
1902-04—Rev. Fred Cromer.
1904-05—Rev. Edward Wettach.
1905-07—Rev. Geo. Welsh.
1908 —Rev. Wm. Yenser.

The church has a membership of 400. Mr. John Houllette is superintendent of the Sabbath school, which has a membership of 470.

1887—The Ladies' Aid of the Grace Reformed church was organized in October, 1887. The present officers of this organization are as follows: Mrs. Wm. Yenser, president; Mrs. Eli Stouffer, vice-president; Mrs. Harry Sponseller, secretary; Mrs. John Roller, corresponding secretary; Mrs. Harvey Rapp, treasurer.

In 1893 the Brotherhood of Andrew and Phillip was organized in the Grace Reformed church October, 1893, with 30 members.

The Lutheran Church

After selling their interest in the Union church built in 1822 we find the Lutheran congregation worshipped in the old Methodist church on East Park avenue. But soon a desire for a building of their own to worship in was agitated. In 1869 a fine brick house of worship was built on the hill in the southern part of the village, which was immediately named "Jerusalem Church." For two long years the people of their faith were longing for a church where they could really feel they were at home. Their membership

Lutheran Church

increased and a comfortable feeling of satisfaction prevailed. The following are the names of the pastors as they continued to fill the pulpit:

1869-74—Rev. S. Baechler.
1874-82—Rev. M. F. Lauffer.
1882-85—Rev. S. Baechler.
1885-95—Rev. A. Birch.

1895 99—Rev. J. H. W. Hoerr.
1899-01—Rev. W. H. Lehman.
1901-09—Rev. G. A. Uber.
1909   —Rev. C. D. Fisher.

The present church Membership numbers 215. Mr. Henry Staley is superintendent of the Sabbath school, which has a membership of 165. Architectural plans have been received for the advisement of remodeling the edifice, which is now too small for their congregation.

Christian Church of Columbiana

December 29, 1876, a temporary organization of seven persons of the Disciple faith was effected by Rev. J. F. Callahan, an evangelist. Until January, 1878, this association met in the school hall, when a permanent organization was formed with the following officers: Elders, David Hoffman and Obadiah Klingingsmith; Deacons, J. M. Williams, George Beck, Peter Wonsetler; Trustees, J. F. Callahan, P. M. Wonsetler, and J. M. Williams. They rented the David Crawford hall on the west side of South Main street and occupied that place as their house of worship until the early '80s, when they abendoned the church indefinitely. In 1879 the membership numbered 23, while the Sunday school enrollment was 45. Rev. Herman Reeves succeeded Rev. J. F. Callahan to the pastorate in April, 1879.

In 1898 a new organization was effected and a place of worship was built on the southwest corner lot of Friend and Middle streets. This is a large frame building and the first officers are as follows:

Rev. Edward Bowers, an evangelist, organized the new church. The pastors of the church are as follows: Rev. E. C. Long, Rev. Linsell, Rev. D. W. Beesaw, Rev. W. M. Crumm, Rev. H. L. Harlow, Rev. E. A. Bosworth, Rev. Ross, Rev. W. A. McCalla, Rev. E. A. Bosworth, 1911, Rev. Alcinous Baker.

Presbyterian Church of Columbiana, Ohio

In May, 1865, the Presbytery of Lisbon, Ohio, granted a petition allowing the privilege of organizing a Presbyterian church in Columbiana, and May 13 such an organization was formed with 16 members. The trustees at this time were: Geo. O. Frasier, J. T. Barclay, and Wm. Gieger. This meeting and several others were held in the school hall. In July, 1865, Mr. Wm. C. Faulkner, a student for the ministry, in their faith, began his ministry in Columbiana. He was ordained to the pastoral office in October, just three months later. In May, 1867, Johnson Campbell and Robert Close were elected elders. This year the present frame church building was erected by Hiram

Presbyterian Church

Bell for the society. During the course of construction a scaffolding insecurely placed fell, killing Thomas Tayler, of Middleton, and severely injuring Joel Morlan, two carpenters at work at the time on this scaffolding, placed there for their use.

The following ministers have served this charge:

    1866-67—Rev. Wm. C. Faulkner.
    1867-68—Rev. John Gilmore.
    1868-70—Rev. J. T. Hall.
    1870-72—Rev. Wm. C. Smith.
    1872-74—Rev. T. P. Johnson.
    1874-85— Rev. A. B. Maxwell.

Rev. Maxwell served this charge as a stated supply, in connection with his pastorate of the church of Leetonia.

The Presbytery, for about a year, furnished supplies to fill vacancy in Columbiana Church.

    1886-88—Rev. R. S. Ravenaugh.   1895-96—Rev. I. S. Hahn.
Again vacancy was filled.   1896-03—Rev. R. E. Porter.
    1889-94—Rev. Isaiah Ravenaugh   1903   —Rev. J. F. Kirkbride.
Vacancy again filled.

G. A. R.

Decoration Day has been observed by the old soldiers and loyal citizens of this town and its environs since the order for its observance was first promulgated by General John A. Logan, commander-in-chief of the G. A. R. Befor the organization of the post, the preliminary work for Decoration Day was performed by committees of soldiers and citizens. Since the organization of the post that work has devolved upon its members and has always been performed in a thorough manner and the best speakers obtainable have always been secured. Following are some of the speakers: 1882, Prof. Taylor of East Palestine, O.; 1883, Hon. L. D. Woodword of Youngstown, O.; 1884, Hon. A. C. Voris of Akron, O.; 1885, Rev. J. V. Lerch of Grace Reformed church; 1886, Hon. P. C. Young of Wellsville, O.; 1887, Rev. Marshall of Lisbon, O.; 1888, Hon. Louis King of Youngstown, O.

Memorial Day has been regularly observed by the post. The members of the post unit with citizens and clergy in holding union services in one of our churches annually, Charity being one of the cardinal principles of the order. James A. Garfield post has contributed liberally for the relief of needy and destitute soldiers, sailors, their widows and orphans. The first recruit to apply for membership after the organization of the post was L. J. Deemer, but James H. Dalzell was first mustered, viz.: December 11, 1881, while L. J. Deemer was mustered December 26, 1881. Harry N. Gates joined January 9, 1882; Wesley Johnston March 23, 1882; J. F. Heacock April 3, 1882; Thos. Piper May 29, 1882; J. F. Woods August 21, 1882; W. S. Weeden September 29, 1882. This was a gain of 8 members during the first year of the organization. A. L. King and A. Sturgeon were mustered October 30, 1882. Next came S. F. Buckley. April 28, 1884, George Lowers was mustered, Wm. L. English September 8, 1884. When the post was three years old they had a membership of 34. Geo. Leaf and Wm. Halverstadt joined October 13; Jno. White November 10, 1884; Geo. Kridler December 28, 1884; J. V. Learch July 28,1885; Geo. A. Jeffries and Henry Williamson, September 14, 1885; Fred Gilbert, Garret Williamson, and Gilbert Williamson, October 3, 1885. John H. Trotter and Nicholous Wining were mustered November 9, 1885; H. H Beck, and Joel Oberholtzer, December 7, 1885. Joseph Hisey joined June 21, 1886. At the end of the fifth year they numbered 51 members. During the sixth year eleven more members joined. They were as follows: Henry Morningstar, Wm. B. Slutter, Wm. Ross, James Bush, Thomas B. Crook, Daniel Strickler, Levi Dickey, Geo. Walters, Joseph Crawford, Robt. 'Scott, Wm. Altaffer E. S. Holloway was re-elected commander at the next election of officers. The commanders who followed him were: Samuel Row, who served two years; I. Bishop, served three years; L. D. Holloway, served two years. The officers longest in continuous service have been Peter Frason, O. M., and Wm. H. Barger, O. D. Both served five years. The growth of the post has been slow but continuous. The largest membership in good standing was 52. The first death in the post was A. Sturgeon, March 15, 1886.

The Columbiana High School

In 1815 a hewed log building was built on a lot where the Grace Reformed church now stands, and in this the first school of our little city was held. In 1822 the building was torn down and no record is had that school was held until 1832, when a frame school building was erected on the southeast corner of Main Cross street, and what is now known as Elm street.

In 1846 this small house of learning was torn down and a one-story brick structure was erected on the site. This building contained two rooms with a hall dividing same, running north and south through the building. A fire utterly destroyed this house in 1860. In June, 1858, District No. 2 was organized under the act of 1853 as a Special District, with Michael Henry, Jacob Greenamyer, and David Woods as a board of education. The board of education in 1862 was as follows: John Icenhour, John Stiver, John Hoke.

Under the advisement of this board the construction of a new school building was commenced. Through some unavoidable cause the structure was not completed until 1864. In the fall of that year the school was again continued under the principalship of Geo. J. Luckey. Mr. Luckey afterwards became superintendent of the Pittsburg schools. This school building was a two-story brick edifice, erected on the northeast corner of Pittsburg street and what is now known as Elm street. It contained three study and two recitation rooms. It was erected on spacious grounds, ornamented with fine trees and shrubbery. In 1873 another building was erected on Vine street at a cost of $12,000. The lower story of this building was divided into three study rooms and the upper story formed a spacious hall for public meetings. These two buildings were quite a distance apart, which made it very unhandy for the principal to properly oversee both schools. It remained in this condition, however, until 1883, when there was erected by the instruction of the board of education, a north addition to the East school building on the corner of Elm and Pittsburg streets.

From 1873 to 1883 the principal was assisted by six teachers. The East and West schools were divided into primary, secondary, intermediate, grammar and high school departments. Each department was graded and candidates for promotion were passed only upon evidence of good scholarship. The number of scholars enrolled in 1879 was 340. These schools were maintained at a cost of about $3,000 per year.

In 1883 the Union school, as it was called for a few years, contained eight study rooms and the superintendent's office. In the basement was two large hot air furnaces which furnished heat to the building in cold weather.

In 1884 Miss Linda Snyder was appointed to the position of principal to take charge of room No. 7 and assist the superintendent in his work. Soon after the county examiners tendered her a life certificate. Her work in our high school was good, commendable and efficient. In the twenty-six years of service in the schools 229 students have graduated through her teachings. Every one of the alumni remembers her with pride, as they think of that careful discipline of the days when studying under her administration. In 1910 she retired from the school cares that had engrossed her attention so long. After about a year of rest she accepted a similar position in the Leetonia schools.

On the 13th day of May, 1909, work was begun razing the south portion of the Union school building, which was built in 1862, and which had at this time been condemned for school purposes. On this site a spacious addition was erected to the remaining north portion, which had been built in 1883. The new building was completed October 1, 1909, at a cost of $25,000. It is a handsome and commodious edifice, a credit to the town and the board of education as well. The board of education is as follows: Jacob Detwiler, president; Henry Staley, clerk; J. M. Webb, I. S. Rauch, and Geo. Holloway. Under the direction of Prof. C. N. McCune the school was continued October 4, 1909, and is now recognized by the state school commissioner and the state high school inspectors as a first grade high school. A diploma from this high school will admit the pupil to any college or university in the state without examination. The school is on the accredited list of the State University, thus placing it on a par with any high school in the state.

The teachers are as follows: Grade 1, Hala Rymer; Grade 2, Edna Johnson; Grade 3, Edna Beard; Grade 4, Annabelle Stooksberry; Grade 5; Edna Fire; Grade 6, Mary Buzard; Grade 7, Olive Phillips; Grade 8, Bessie Rice· High school teachers: Principal, Hurd A. Tuttle, teaching science and mathematics; Jean S. Garrard, teaching Latin and German; Ethel Sprague, teaching English and history; Supt. C. N. McCune, teaching history and commercial branches. A new teacher to teach music and some high school work is yet to be employed. The new addition is divided as follows: four rooms given to grade work, four are given exclusively to high school work, two play rooms in the basement, and the superintendent's office on the second floor.

The total enrollment is 446.

The two highest Patterson graduates in the county last year came from Columbiana. The teachers have all had some normal training.

The school is maintained at about $10,000 per year.

The accompaning picture is from a photograph of the Columbiana High School's first basketball team. It was organized for the season of 1911-12. Bottom row, left to right, we have: Allen Heston, Thomas Harrold, Samuel Rogers, John Robinson, captain; Norman Detwiler, Maurice White, Hurd A. Tuttle, coach; Will Krayer, manager.

First Basketball Team

High School Graduates.

Following is a list of graduates from the Columbiana high school since the first year the pupils were graduated.

Class of 1881—Estella Jamison, Charles Esterly.

Class of 1883—Edward Esterly, Oliver Haas, John Fitzpatrick, Harry Allen, George A. Smith, Lena Hayden.

Class of 1885—Clement H. Miller, Henry Staley, Frank H. Roninger, Wm. L. Esterly, W. H. Hayden, S. S. Snyder, Jesse Allen, Robert Esterly, Kate Koch, Ola Esterly.

Class of 1886—Howard Keyser, Nora Havil, Martha Kircher, Mollie A. Buzard, S. V. Rohrbaugh, Francis E. Bailey, Margaret M. Strickler.

Class of 1887—Mazie Smith, Frank J. Deemer, Harvey S. Firestone, Ella U. Bushong, Charles M. Rohrbaugh, Loma M. Keyser, L. I. Snyder, Della A. Mellinger, W. G. Strickler, Harriet H. Shields, Edgar M. Vogleson, Chas. L. West, Ida L. Bomesberger.

Class of 1888—Franzo D. Miller, Della A. Fisher, John Vogleson, Mary E. Vogleson, Mary E. DeHoff, Harriet B. Esterly, Chas. D. Strickler, Cora B. Roninger, Ida B. Bushong.

Class of 1889—Chas. Halverstadt, Park H. Weaver, George M. Overholt, Jennie M. Buckley, J. Ross Flickinger, Frank Sponseller, Kittie B. Allen, Jesse J. Haas, Horace C. Jones, Geo. M. Todd, Geo. A. Esterly, Frank H. Grove, M. Tullius Inman, Jade L. King.

Class of 1890—Ada E. Halverstadt, Effie J. Rohrbaugh, Luella M. Metz.

Class of 1891—May Halverstadt, Mame Overholtzer, Lizzie D. Flickinger, Robert J. Firestone.

Class of 1892—Ida J. Calvin, Blanche Miller, Ida L. Tullis, Josie Sample, Rhoda Halverstadt, Eta B. Beardsley, Maud C. Johnson, Ella M. Johnson, Edwin R. Birch.

Class of 1893—Tillie Gieger, Harry E. Esterly, Edwin L. Rickert, Chas. S. Todd, S. S. Lipply, Chas. T. Ink, Dora B. Inman.

Class of 1894—Mary A. Marlatt, Walter W. Shriver.

Class of 1895—Elizabeth F. Alexander, L. Blanche Beard, Clement Beard, Lizzie Doty, Clark M. Flohr, Fred A. Inman, Mayme M. Ink, Nettie C. Keister, Elizabeth Stauffer, Myrtle Zellars.

Class of 1896—Ida Maud Alexander, May Anglemyer, Kathryn C. Brickman, Emma D. Detrow, F. Mabel Read, Minnie E. Weaver, Herbert H. Halverstadt, Walter C. McGaffick, Albert Birch, John H. Nold.

Class of 1897—Harriet B. Detwiler, Ella B. Flickinger, Margaret B. Harrold, M. Eleanor Nevin, Anna M. Nold, Ella M. Staley, Edna G. Witt, Robert M. Bomesberger, Edwin H. Detwiler, Ceder J. Renkenberger.

Class of 1898—Walter N. Bomesberger, Grace A. Greenamyer, Elizabeth MacIntosh, C. M. Smith, Dallas C. Sitler, Harry E. Detwiler, Frank H. Shilling, Mary L. Kreyer, Grace G. Hisey.

Class of 1899—Ada B. DeVere, Grace Flickinger, Mary Halverstadt, Stella Kuegle, Cora E. Miller, Hala Rymer, Ida Matilda Staley, John Heckler, Jesse Rupert, Walter Sample, Harry Troll.

Class of 1900—Stella Beard, Mame Flickinger, Paul Greenamyer, Alice Harrold, Paul Kuegle, Homer Lehman, Edna McGaffick, Thomas Rymer, Harvey Shilling.

Class of 1901—Harvey Beck, Walter W. Beck, Edgar Bell, Lucile Bonnette, Edith Rose Heck, W. D. Holloway, Chas. Keller, Clifford Lehman, Fred B. Nold, Harvey I. Rickett, Edna Renkenberger, Jeanette Shaffer, Irvin Sample, Arthur D. Tidd.

Class of 1902—Mabelle B. Caughey, Leon L. Houlette, Ralph F. Keller, Earl M. McCurry, Aldine G. Metzler, Iva G. Renkenberger, Clarence Rupert, Roy E. Weaver, Vera W. Windle.

Class of 1903—Leroy P. Holloway, Ada A. Houk, Pearl M. Bushong, Leila F. Beard, Dortha McGinnis, Otta G. Orr.

Class of 1904—Josephine O. Beck, Bertha Esterly, Elsie L. Harrold, Lois J. Halverstadt, Blanche E. Smith, Elva A. Houk, Katie Shriver, Blanche M. Rupert, Willis Shontz.

Class of 1905—Edna Fire. Lloyd Wilson.

Class of 1906—Selma Brown, F. Ray Fitzpatrick, John T. Fitzsimmons, Nina Mae Inman, . Wilbur Koch, Albert S. Kuegle, Irwin F. Moyer, Ada Isaphene Rupert, Hazel Lillian.

Class of 1907—Pauline Esther Myers, Carrie Belle Munson, Mae Munson, Mary Ethel Hisey, Dick Fitzpatrick.

Class of 1908—Carrie Harrold, Robert Culp, Elben Lehman, Hattie Hyland, Olive Russell, Cora Fisher, Mabel Wining, Lucile Breckenridge, Leo Holloway.

Class of 1909—Chloe Elizabeth Houk, Olive Mae Esterly, Alverta Louis Houk, Helen Loretta Greenamyer.

Class of 1910—Leota H. Astry, Edna I. Beard, Rhoda M. Beatty, Ola M. DeRhodes, Estella G. Esterly, Lois H. Fire, Lawrence Flickinger, Erma R. Frederick, Mae K. Frye, Louis M. Hart, Nella M. Koch, Irma Kohler, Karl Kreyer, Ethel A. Lenning, Geo. McMillan, Orlando T. McGaffick, Elsie E. Miller, Clara E. Owens, Clarence Shontz, Vera F. Theiss, Theodore Theiss, John L. Ward, Clara M. White, Adam M. Woolf, Howard Zellars.

Class of 1911—Olive Theiss, Erma R. Esterly, Hazel M. Fuhrman, Eleanor R. Theiss, Mary Ethel Esterly, Ethel S. Todd, Orania Mae Might.

Class of 1912—Cora L. Esterly, Erma G. Grove, Lena M. Grossen, Sue G. Harrold, Kathryn L. Myers, Givah M. Newell, Olive M. Shontz, Cora M. Smith, Arden R. Basinger, Wilbur DeRhodes, Will Krayer, Adin L. Miller, Howard R. Orr, Maurice D. White.

Alumni of Columbiana High School

On the evening of September 9, 1885, an organization of the Alumni of the Columbiana High School was effected.

The opening meeting of this association was had at the home of Miss Ola Esterly, September 3, 1885. Eleven members were present and Mr. George Smith was elected chairman pro. tem., and Miss Lena Hayden was appointed secretary pro. tem. At this meeting Mr. Harry Allen, Mr. Sylvanus Snyder and Miss Lena Hayden were appointed a committee to draft a constitution and by-laws.

At the next meeting, held September 9, 1885, the constitution and by-laws were received and committee discharged. A permanent organization was then effected. The first elected officers are as follows: President, Chas. E. Esterly; vice-president, Ola Esterly; secretary, Lena Hayden; treasurer, Frank Roninger; sergeant-at-arms, John Fitzpatrick.

Alumni's second meeting was held in 1886.

Alumni's third meeting was held in 1904.

Alumni's fourth meeting was held in 1906.

Then annual meetings were held about commencement times with increasing interest.

The 1912 officers of Columbiana High School Alumni are as follows: President, John T. Fitzsimmons; vice-president, Roy E. Weaver; secretary, Theodore Theiss; treasurer, Irvin Moyer.

The city of Columbiana has had other societies now and again, chiefly of the nature of temperance, musical, and literary associations.

Columbiana's Business Directory

ATTORNEYS
H. W. Hammond, Main St.
W. O. Wallace, Main St.

BAKERS
Harry Lautenschlager, Pittsburg St.

BANKS
The Union Banking Co., Main St.

BARBERS
E. S. Coblentz, Main St.
Evans & Coleman, Union St.

BASKET FACTORY
David Beard, Lisbon St.

BLACKSMITHS
John V. Esterly, Friend St.
Harvey Harrold, East Park Ave.
Warren Roller, Elm St.
D. B. Wilkinson, Main St.

BOILER MAKERS
Columbiana Boiler Co., Railroad St.

BOOKS AND STATIONERY
W. L. Augustine, Main St.

BUTCHERS
Buzard and Shontz, Main St.
Wm. Wagonhouser, Main St.

CARRIAGE MAKERS AND DEALERS
Zimmer and Harmon, corner Walnut and Vine Alleys.

COAL DEALERS
Curtis Stahl, East Park Ave.

COMMISSION MERCHANTS
Harry E. Detwiler, Main St.
Sylvanus Hisey, North Main St.
U. Shillinger and Son, Main St.
James Windle, farmer, east of town.

COOPERS
Wm. Fesler, farmer, east of town.
Wm. Haag, Union St.
Eli Hisey, farmer, north of town.
Harry Shauber, farmer, west of town.

DAIRY
Henry Cole, Eastern Dairy, east of town.
N. S. Hart, south of town.
Frank Poulton, southeast of town.

DENTISTS
W. S. Baker, Main St.
P. H. Felger, Public Square.

DRESSMAKERS
Mrs. M. A. Munson, North Main St.

DRUGGISTS
C. B. Clapp & Co., Main St.
H. B. Law, Main St.
Ed. Lodge, Main St.

DRY GOODS
Fire & Co., Main St.
W. T. Holloway, Main St.
F. D. Lodge, Main St.
Tidds, Main St.

ELECTRICAL CONTRACTOR
F. S. Lennig, Union St.

ENTERPRISE MFG. CO.
Jacob Detwiler, Railroad St.

EXPRESS COMPANIES
Adams Express Co., Main St.
Wells Fargo & Co., Pittsburg St.

FARM IMPLEMENTS
J. W. Hively, Main St.

FEED AND GRAIN
Brungard Milling Co., Elm St.
Coyle Bros., Railroad St.
Albert Esterly, Friend St.
S. S. Weaver, Main St.

FOUNDRIES
The Columbiana Foundry, west of S. Main St.
Wm. Lauten's Brass Foundry, South Main St.

FRUIT HOUSE
Harry Detwiler, Friend St.

FURNITURE
Vaughn Bros., Main St.

GARAGE AND REPAIR SHOPS
The Auto Machine Co., East Park Ave.
Henry Theiss, Elm St.

GARMENT FACTORY
The Duquesne Mfg. Co., Railroad St.

GENTS' FURNISHINGS
Shasteen & Fitzpatrick Bros., Main St.

CLOTHIERS, TAILORS, FURNISHERS
Chas. E. Smith, Main St.

GREENHOUSES
Henry Weaver North Main St.

GROCERIES
Buzard & Shontz, Main St.
J. A. Crawford, Main St.
J. J. Fesler, Main St.
F. E. Sitler, Main St.
J. B. Stouffer, Main St.

HANDLE FACTORY AND CEMENT WORKS
The Columbiana Mfg. Co., corner Railroad and Middle Sts.

HARDWARE
H. A. Keller, Main St.
Lehman & Shaffer, Main St.

HOTELS
Hotel Krohmer, South Main St.
Park House, Public Square
Troll House, Main St.

ICE FACTORY
F. E. Sitler, Main St.

INSURANCE AND REAL ESTATE
Kenty & Albright, Main St.

JUSTICES OF THE PEACE
S. S. Weaver, Main St.
Philip Theiss, Public Square.

JEWELERS
P. M. Koch, Main St.
Tidd & Son, Main St.

LAUNDRY
Lee Soon, Main St.

LIVERY STABLES
H. W. Beck, corner Spring and Walnut alleys.
B. Bowman & Son, Elm St.
Fred J. McGahan, Main St.
Sawyer & McGahan, Park Ave.

LUMBER YARDS
Columbiana Lumber Co., Union St.

MARBLE WORKS
Isaiah Flickinger, Main St.

MASONS
George Bear, Elm St.
Robert Chestnut, Main St.

FLOUR MILL
Brungard Milling Co., Elm St.

MILLINERS
Mrs. F. F. Garrett, Main St.
Miss Carrie Munson, Main St.
Tidd's, Main St.

MUSIC INSTRUCTORS
Miss Emma Koenreich, Main St.
Miss Estella Kuegle, Main St.
Homer Troll, North Main St.

NEWSPAPER DEALER
John Ryan, Main St.

NOTARY PUBLIC
H. W. Hammond, Main St.
W. O. Wallace, Main St.
S. S. Weaver, Main St.

ODD JOB SHOP
W. W. Wolfgang, West Park Ave.

PHOTO PLAY
J. M. Webb, Main St.

PHOTOGRAPHERS
E. H. Berlin, Main St.
J. M. Webb, Main St.

PHYSICIANS
G. H. Albright, Main St.
Harry Bookwalter, Main St.
J. A. Mellon, Main St.
A. C. Tidd, Main St.

PLASTERERS
John Baer, East Park Ave.
Joseph King, Elm St.
Adam Wise, Main St.

PIPE FITTERS
W. W. Wolfgang, West Park Ave.

PLUMBERS
Lehman & Shaffer, Main St.
Harvey Rapp, Duquesne St.

POOL ROOMS
John Baer, Main St.
J. R. McDonald, Thomas Bldg., Main St.

JOB PRINTERS
G. Ernest Koch, Elm St.
Ledger Printing Co., Public Square.

PUMP WORKS
The Columbiana Pump Co.

RACKET STORES
Wm. Basler, Main St.
G. B. Keyser, Main St.
Hesketh's 5 & 10 Cent Store, Pub. Sq.

REAL ESTATE AGENTS
Royal Conkey, Elm St.
J. M. Irons, Main St.
M. A. Wint, Elm St.

RESTAURANTS
T. J. Greer, Main St.
Wm. Lauten, Main St.

SADDLES AND HARNESS
W. R. Knowles, Main St.
Fred Thoman, Main St.

SHOE DEALERS
Jeffreys Bros., Main St.
Rauch & Hartman, Main St.

STOVES AND TINWARE
John Beard, Main St.

MERCHANT TAILORS
James Agnew, cor. Main and Friend St.
Henry Imig, Main St.

TINNERS AND SLATEROOFERS
George Astry, Friend St.
John Beard, Main St.
Snauffer & Hum, Main at end of Union
W. W. Wolfgang, West Park Ave.

TOOL MANUFACTURER AND GENERAL BLACKSMITH
Harvey Harrold, East Park Ave.

UNDERTAKER
Raymond Vaughn, Main St.
Albert McCormick, Main St.

VETERANARY SURGEON
Dr. W. O. McGuigan, West Park Ave.

WEEKLY NEWSPAPER
Columbiana Ledger, Public Square.

WAGON MAKER
David Beard, Lisbon St.

www.ingramcontent.com/pod-product-compliance
Lightning Source LLC
Chambersburg PA
CBHW030346100526
44592CB00010B/855